On God's Existence

Traditional and New Arguments

John J. Pasquini

Hamilton Books

An Imprint of
Rowman & Littlefield
Lanham • Boulder • New York • Toronto • Plymouth, UK

Copyright © 2016 by Hamilton Books
4501 Forbes Boulevard, Suite 200, Lanham, Maryland 20706
Hamilton Books Acquisitions Department (301) 459-3366

Unit A, Whitacre Mews, 26-34 Stannary Street,
London SE11 4AB, United Kingdom

Library of Congress Control Number: 2016935008
ISBN: 978-0-7618-6765-4 (pbk : alk. paper)—ISBN: 978-0-7618-6766-1 (electronic)

♾️™ The paper used in this publication meets the minimum requirements of American National Standard for Information Sciences Permanence of Paper for Printed Library Materials, ANSI/NISO Z39.48-1992.

Contents

Praise for John J. Pasquini

"John Pasquini's *On God's Existence* is a remarkably inclusive journey through the maze of arguments, proofs, and demonstrations that have engaged the intellectual and spiritual energies of the best minds in Western civilization. From Thomas Aquinas to Descartes, Newman, C.S. Lewis and other recent philosophers and theologians. Pasquini's elegant and sober, yet insightfully critical and profound discussion of both classic and modern representatives of the debate on God invites the reader to join the conversation, to become a participant, not just an observer, in this most important of all conversations. Scholarly, compelling, critical – a work I regard as indispensable to anyone who dares to ask the fundamental questions about the ultimate sense of human life."

　　—*Sixto J. Garcia, PhD., Emeritus Professor of Systematic and Philosophical Theology, Notre Dame, Formerly, St. Vincent de Paul Regional Seminary.*

"The phenomenon of the existence of God has been a central and continuing preoccupation in Western Christian tradition. Fr. Pasquini's contribution to the probability of this existence is a seminal, comprehensive and persuasive text. In each succinct chapter, Pasquini reports and advances the scholarship of this mystery. The discussions involving consciousness and stunted psychological development are particularly compelling psychologically-based arguments. Truly an invaluable tool in presenting exhaustive views of the inquiry."

　　—*Wayne L. Creelman, MD, MTS, DLFAPA, Psychiatry/Psychology, McCabe Professor and Eminent Scholar, University of Florida School of Medicine.*

"In our time many people assume that belief in God is not knowledge, but merely a subjective preference or attitude, which cannot be demonstrated through rational, logical reasoning. But in his newly released book, *On God's Existence: Traditional and New Arguments*, Fr. John Pasquini presents a concise yet comprehensive summary of logical arguments that discredit this false and, ultimately disastrous, assumption. By approaching the question of God's existence from a great variety of perspectives, he shows that belief in God is actually far more reasonable and logical than its rejection."

—*G. Alexander Ross, Ph.D., Sociology, Institute of Psychological Science, Professor Emeritus.*

"Fr. Pasquini book *On God's Existence* presents excellent logical arguments to prove the presence of God. He uses great examples from scientists, philosophers, and theologians to validate his case. As a Catholic as well as a scientist, it is nice to have these arguments presented to help us who believe defend our faith . . . ."

—*Jonathan Volk, Ph. D., Natural Sciences/Chemical Engineer, formerly at Quantum Technology Sciences, Northrop Grumman Corp.; currently a research scientist at the Center for the Advancement of Science in Space (CASIS).*

"The book *On God's Existence* is a fascinating work that is sure to enrich the lives of those who read it. Touching on a variety of contemporary topics in the realm of the faith, *On God's Existence* will challenge the reader to go deeper into the "proofs" of the existence of God, and to realize the many ways that one can embark in order to arrive at the same conclusion: God is real, God is true, and God walks with us on every step of this human existence. I highly recommend this book to all those wishing to grow in the faith and understanding of the greatest mystery of the universe: God's Existence."

—*Rev. Dr. Alfred Cioffi, S.T.D., Ph.D., Professor of Biology and Bioethics, Blue Cross-Shield Endowed Chair in Bioethics in STEM, St. Thomas University; National Catholic Bioethics Center, Consultant.*

"It was a delight to read Father Pasquini"s masterful summary of centuries of great arguments (and a few new ones!) for the existence of God. In modern times we seem to have lost the gift for sound reasoning, such as displayed in every chapter here in clear and even pithy ways by the author. Further, it is a great tragedy that so few of our young people anymore are exposed to the multiple converging and compelling logical bases of the near inescapable necessity to posit a Divine Creator. Should we then be so surprised that so few of our youth are now firm and confident believers? A book like this one is in perpetual need in every age – over and over a new generation must learn anew the basic truths so well defended by a powerful set of arguments which Father Pasquini so ably offers on nearly every page."

—*Richard E. Gallagher, M.D., Professor of Clinical Psychiatry, New York Medical College; faculties, Columbia University and St. Joseph's Seminary (Director of Psychological Services).*

"We look to the heavens and are in awe of what we envision. What wonder . . . what majesty . . . how can there not be a God. But then reason begins to taunt us . . . and we question. *On God's Existence* takes one through the classical "proofs" and gathers exciting modern scientific approaches to these arguments for the Creator. With this little gem, Fr. John Pasquini shares with us 33 succinctly wrapped posits, converging on that which brings meaning and purpose to existence. In so doing, his frequent personal "asides" summon many of the questions that arise in each of us as we engage these thoughtful passages."

—*The Very Rev. Paul E. Mottl, M.R.E., M.Div., Th.D., Ph.D., Dean, Providence Theological School, Ret. Canon to the Ordinary for the Episcopal Diocese of Pennsylvania.*

"This book is a good tool especially for those seeking the truth about God's existence. Fr. John J. Pasquini renders a valuable service by succinctly presenting the many varied theories about the existence and non-existence of God. This book provokes both one's thought and reflection. In a world where many want to reduce the question of God to the private and sentimental sphere, this book comes as a providential asset to state that God endowed the human person with intelligence not to forgo it [but to use it] in our pursuance of Him."

—*Rev. Dr. Nicholas Cachia S.T.D., Associate Professor, Theology/Philosophy, St Vincent de Paul Regional Seminary.*

"Although already a believer and forever a man of science, I still find inspiration and life in Fr. Pasquini's treatment of that which, from time immemorial, has delighted as many as it has confounded. This book, which I recommend with enthusiasm, is clearly the work of an inspired and knowledgeable evangelizer."

—*Fr. Chamindra Williams, Ph.D., Mathematics/Chemistry, Adjunct Professor of Palm Beach State College.*

"From the time of creation, we have desired to know and explain the Creator. In this compendium of reasonable arguments, Fr. Pasquini offers a thorough re-examination of this question. It is my hope that many "searchers" will find reasons to believe and give greater meaning to their lives."

—_Monsignor David L. Toups, S.T.D., Theology/Philosophy, Rector/President, St. Vincent de Paul Regional Seminary._

"Pasquini's work echoes from page to page the crux of Einstein's spirit who claimed, "Everyone who is seriously engaged in the pursuit of science becomes convinced that the laws of nature manifest the existence of a spirit vastly superior to that of men." Pasquini's work is succinct, precise, and ingenious. It echoes his deep seated belief that atheism is more a malady (atheist Personality disorder) than an intellectual movement."

—_Florence Traversy, Ph.D., Physics/Natural Sciences, École Normale Nicolet, Professor Emeritus._

"This wonderful piece of writing has [explored] the questions that man has sought [answers] to since the beginning of time . . . . This book, well written and researched, should be on the shelf of any [believer], especially enabling the reader to refute the many mistruths that are encountered each day."

—_Rev. D. Brian Horgan, M.Div., MS., MSW (I)., Ph.D., Psychology, Northcentral University._

Introduction

For many, the existence or non-existence of God will never be able to be proved or disproved, for that would require a mind capable of all knowledge, of all reality in every dimension. The human mind is finite in its capacity to function, and therefore could never be all-knowing.

For Catholics, the natural light of human reason—even if limited—is capable of coming to a knowledge of God. Others, however, disagree.

Given the disagreements, the question for our endeavor must be, therefore: Is God's existence more or less probable than his non-existence? That is, what are the most converging and convincing arguments for the existence or non-existence of God?

Philosophy and the advances in cosmology, neurology, molecular biology, and the social sciences have made the convincing and converging arguments for God's existence more probable than ever before in history.

In every inquiry, we must begin, according to Aristotle's maxim, with what we know first and best—ourselves. This maxim is what makes the arguments for the existence of God over his non-existence more favorable. Or in the thoughts of Francis Bacon, more in conformity to the laws of thought.

The following arguments are updated and revised versions of classic or traditional arguments as well as new arguments resulting from the advances in the modern sciences. While not all the philosophers of the arts and sciences could be explicitly cited—in reference to the almost innumerable arguments, pro and con—the following text is so fashioned as to take into account the hundreds of variant arguments that have been implicitly and explicitly expounded over the years. This is so particularly when the entire text is understood as a whole argument, subdivided into several component arguments—that is, the complementarity of all the following arguments form a single argument—like pieces to a puzzle.

1
AQUINAS' ARGUMENTS FROM CHANGE AND CAUSES (ARISTOTELIAN INFLUENCED ARGUMENTS)

Colloquially speaking, in regards to the universe, "What is the 'thing' that began it all and keeps it going?"

A series of closely placed upright dominoes will remain standing until someone or something makes one domino fall onto another. Then the cascade of falling dominoes begins. Someone or something had to cause the first domino to fall, to begin the cascade. Someone or something had to change the position of the first domino for the others to fall. Without a first cause or first cause of change, all remains standing silently, motionless . . . . What is said of dominoes is so with the universe in its multiplicity of causes and changes.

Aquinas' first argument goes as follows:

> The first and most obvious way [to prove the existence of God] is based on change. We see things changing. Anything that changes is being changed by something else. . . . This something else, if itself changing, is being changed by yet another thing; and this last change by another. Now we must stop somewhere, otherwise there will be no first cause of the change, and, as a result, no subsequent causes. (Only when acted upon by a first cause do intermediate causes produce a change. . . .) We arrive then at some first cause of change not itself being changed by anything, and this is what everybody understands by God. [1]

The philosopher Peter Kreeft summarizes Aquinas' argument in the following manner: "Since no thing (or series of things) can move (change) itself, there must be a first, Unmoved Mover, source of all motion." [2]

Either change in the universe is characterized by an unending, eternally preceding series of causes of change (an infinite regress without a first cause), or there is an ultimate first cause of change (a finite regress). Since everything in our human experience seems to affirm the logic of an ultimate cause of change, logic favors a first uncaused cause for change in the universe—which we call God.

The idea of an infinite regress is counterintuitive. Human intuition imparts in us that all regressions are finite. The sense that there is a first uncaused cause of change is an innate sense found in healthy individuals, and innate senses of "things" correspond to reality. [3]

The nature of the causes of change or motion makes God's existence more likely than his non-existence. But what exactly is this uncaused cause of change, this first cause of change not itself being changed, this unmoved mover, that we call God? Let us look at the following example first.

Aquinas' second argument is similar to his first. It is based on the very notion of causation.

> The second way [to prove the existence of God] is based on the very notion of cause. In the observable world causes derive their causality from other causes; we never observe, nor ever could, something causing itself, for this would mean it preceded itself, and this is not possible. But the deriving of causality must stop somewhere; for in the series of causes an earlier member causes an intermediate and the intermediate a last (whether the intermediate be one or many). Now eliminate a cause and you also eliminate its effects: you cannot have a last cause, nor an intermediate one, unless you have a first. Given . . . no first cause, there will be no intermediate causes and no last effect; which contradicts observation. So one is forced to suppose some first cause, to which everyone gives the name of God.[4]

Kreeft summarizes this argument by Aquinas as follows: "Nothing can cause its own existence. If there is no first, uncaused cause of the chain of causes and effects we see, these second causes could not exist. They do, so IT must."[5]

Either cause in the universe is characterized by an unending, eternally preceding series of causes (an infinite regress of causes), or there is an ultimate first uncaused cause to subsequent causes (a finite regress). Since everything in our human experience seems to affirm the logic of an ultimate cause for subsequent causes, logic favors a first cause, and this first uncaused cause is what we call God.

As cited in the first argument, the idea of an infinite regress is counterintuitive. Human intuition imparts in us that all regressions are finite. The sense that there must be a first cause to subsequent causes is an innate sense found in healthy individuals, and innate senses of "things" correspond to reality.

The existence of God over his non-existence is more probable due to the features of change and causation—and our experience of them.

What is it that can be considered as being an uncaused cause of change, a first cause of change not itself being changed, an unmoved mover, a cause without a cause? To go further, what can be considered a sustainer of existence without needing a sustainer, a being not susceptible to an infinite regress problem, a being not bound by space and time? The only answer is *existence itself, subsistent existence.* And *existence itself* is another name for "I AM," God. *Subsistent existence* excludes an infinite regress.

An Aside

When speaking of existence itself, subsistent existence, we are speaking about that which gives existence, sustains existence, and yet is independent to what it sustains and gives existence to.

2

THE BIG BANG

The more I examine the universe and study the details of its architecture, the more evidence I find that the universe in some sense knew we were coming.[6]
—Freeman Dyson, Physicist and Mathematician

As to the first cause of the universe . . . that is for the [individual] to insert, but our picture is incomplete without Him.[7]
—Edward Milne, Astrophysicist, Mathematician

The big bang marks the beginning of matter, energy, space and time.[8]

The big bang of primordial stuff or ylem occurred approximately 13.8 billion years ago. After the initial big bang and corresponding expansion, the universe cooled sufficiently to allow energy to be converted into protons, neutrons, and electrons. The expanding and cooling universe developed into gravitational, electromagnetic, strong and weak nuclear forces, and what would eventually become our modern conception of the universe.

The great dilemma with the big bang theory is that it cannot explain what happened before it. Where did this compact, dense primordial stuff or ylem come from and what caused it to explode?

The theory of the oscillating universe (or variations of it) is an alternative to the traditional big bang theory. This theory argues that after the big bang—the beginning--the universe expanded and will continue to expand to a point where it can no longer expand (due to the universe's density or concentration of mass); once this point of expansion has reached its capacity, the universe's expansion will eventually stop and the universe will begin contracting until it collapses back into its original primordial state, preparing to explode and expand again. Thus the universe, according to this theory, is seen as continually expanding and contracting, continually oscillating, with no end—after an initial big bang beginning.

Another possibility is that there was never a beginning to the big bang. That is, the universe always existed as an oscillating universe.

If the world had a beginning, an initial big bang, then what caused it? Furthermore, what is the source of the material that made the big bang possible?

If the world had no beginning—or an initial big bang with an eternal cycling--(i.e., eternally oscillating, cycling or bouncing—which is for some problematic in terms of the second law of thermodynamics or the Borde-Vilenkin-Guth Theorem)[9] the convergence of probabilities still favors God: An oscillating universe is made up of things. What keeps these things in existence or is the source of these things?

Only what we would call God, in all likelihood, can be the first cause or prime mover if there is a beginning. And if there is no beginning, then only what we call God, in all likelihood, could be the sustainer of the existence of a continually oscillating world.

Regarding the first point, all things that exist in our sphere of comprehension exist because someone or something put it into existence. And in terms of an always existing, oscillating universe, human experience teaches us that something that exists needs something to sustain it in existence?

What therefore is it that can be considered as being a cause without a cause, a sustainer of existence without needing a sustainer, a being not susceptible to an infinite regress problem, a being not bound by space and time? The only answer is—as seen in chapter one--existence itself, subsistent existence. And existence itself is another name for God.

Either the world always existed, or God always existed. Either God was the source of the big bang or the beginning of being, or something else.

Logic favors God. The most convincing and converging argument favors the existence of God over his non-existence in regards to the big bang.[10] This is intuitive.

An Aside I

Scientists currently hold to a beginning for the "big bang." They also hold to the idea that prior to the "big bang" there was no space and time. The question: What existed prior to the "big bang"? Something cannot come from nothing. So what is this "something"? And what is this "something" not bound by space and time? The only phenomenon that can be postulated is existence itself, subsistent existence. And this is what we call God!

An Aside II

Reiterating an important point from Chapter One, when speaking of existence itself, subsistent existence, we are speaking about that which gives existence, sustains existence, and yet is independent to what it sustains and gives existence to.

3
THE TIME ARGUMENT

The time argument, often referred to as the *kalam* argument, is based on a variation of Aquinas' arguments from change and causation.

Scientists argue that prior to the big bang time did not exist. Time began with the big bang some thirteen to twenty billion years ago, they argue. This big bang gave rise to the first moment, which gave rise to all the other moments.

The question: What existed prior to the big bang that was not in time and yet was the cause of the big bang that gave rise to time? Experience favors God over any other reality. This is logically intuitive.

Logic favors subsistent existence, existence itself, which is the fullness of time, the actuality of time, the eternal now, a reality beyond the constraints of time—from which time finds it origin. We call this subsistent existence God.

Time's origins makes the likelihood of God's existence more likely than less likely.[11]

An Aside

Could time always have existed? Either time is characterized by an unending, eternally preceding series of moments (an infinite regress) or there is an ultimate beginning to time, the first moment for all subsequent moments (a finite regress). Since everything in our human experience has an ultimate beginning, so too, it can be presumed for time. An infinite regress is counter-intuitive. That there is a beginning to time is an innate belief. Innate beliefs, in a healthy individual, correspond to reality.

Finally, since time is simply another word for change, Aquinas' argument regarding change applies here as well.

The existence of time makes the likelihood of God's existence more likely than less likely.

4
ORIGIN OF LIFE

After one can overcome the challenge of how to produce life from non-life,
living matter from non-living matter, then one must explain . . . the emergence
of life-forms with a capacity for reproducing themselves? Without the existence of such a capacity, it would not have been possible for different species
to emerge through random mutation and natural selection." [These biological
phenomena] provide us with reason for doubting that it is possible to account
for existent life-forms in purely materialistic [atheistic] terms and without
recourse to design. [12]
—David Conway, Scientist/ Philosopher of Science

That there is indeed a limit upon science is made very likely by the existence
of questions that science cannot answer, and that no conceivable advance of
science would empower it to answer . . . . I have in mind such questions as:
How did everything begin? What are we all here for? What is the point of
living? [13]
—Nobel Prize Winner, Peter Medawar, Oxford Immunologist

What are some of the theories on the origin of life? [14]

Life is believed to have begun approximately 3.7 billion years ago in a
primordial soup—a water based sea of simple organic molecules. The problem: Science has not been able to prove that a primordial soup existed, and if
it did, the conditions of the earth's early atmosphere would not have made
life possible in such a soup.

Geochemists argue that the early earth's atmosphere was likely highly
volcanic and largely composed of carbon dioxide rather than a mixture of
reducing gases like methane, ammonia and hydrogen, and thus not conducive
to life.

The origin of life theorist, David Deamer (echoing the work of his colleagues), argues that the early earth's atmosphere did not support the necessary array of "synthetic pathways leading to possible monomers." [15] (A
monomer is a molecule that reacts chemically to another molecule of the
same type to form a larger molecule.)

Without the building blocks to life, life cannot exist!

In 2010 the biochemist Nick Lane argued for life arising from undersea
hydrothermal vents. The difficulty with this theory—as in the case of the
primordial soup theory--is that it fails to adequately explain how amino acids
or other molecules link up to form polymers in a non-conducive, soupy, wet
environment. A primordial soup or undersea hydrothermal vent would seem
to break down protein chains rather than build them up. [16]

Without the building blocks of life, life cannot exist!

If we assume that complex organic molecules could somehow have been
formed, then they would have had to somehow develop the ability to repli-

cate. Those complex molecules best suited to replicate would then have needed to be naturally selected for survival. These molecules would eventually have needed to have evolved complex machinery to insure survival and reproduction. What are the chances?

Life on earth is estimated to have begun approximately 3.7 billion years ago. The probabilities of life occurring by chance, without divine assistance, is essentially impossible from a statistical point of view—given the 3.7 billion years. The odds of a single cell evolving, never mind a human being, in 3.7 billion years has been estimated by statisticians at 1.6 followed by 59 zeros to one. A statistical miracle!

> An honest man, armed with all the knowledge available to us now, could only state that in some sense, the origin of life appears at the moment to be almost a miracle, so many are the conditions which would have had to have been satisfied to get it going. [17]
> —Francis Crick, Atheist Co-discoverer of the DNA Double Helix

> More than 30 years of experimentation on the origin of life in the field of chemical and molecular evolution have led to a better perception of the immensity of the problem of the origin of life on earth rather than to its solution. At present all discussions on principle theories and experiments in the field [end up] in a confession of ignorance. [18]
> —Klaus Dose, President of Biochemistry, University of Johannes Gutenberg

> What creates life out of the inanimate compounds that make up living things? No one knows. How were the first organisms assembled? Nature hasn't given us the slightest tint. If anything, the mystery has deepened over time. [19]
> —Greg Easterbrook, Science Writer

In summary, non-living materials cannot produce living materials. A universe of mindless, non-living materials cannot produce living beings with intrinsic ends, self-replicating capabilities, and a coded chemistry. [20] Life is brought about by life, by preexisting life structures.

Human experience demonstrates to us that when we find design we can find a designer, when we find order we can find an orderer, and when we find a beginning we can find an originator.

In regards to the origin of life dilemma, God as the designer, orderer, originator is favored over chance, coincidence, or synchronicity. This is logically intuitive.

God's existence is favored over his non-existence. [21]

5

AQUINAS' ARGUMENT FROM EXISTENCE ITSELF

The philosopher Leibniz once wrote: "The first question which should rightly be asked is this: why is there something rather than nothing?"

> The [argument from existence] is based on what need not be and on what must be.... Some of the things we come across can be but need not be, for we find them springing up and dying away, thus sometimes in being sometimes not. Now everything cannot be like this, for a thing that need not be, once was not; and if everything need not be, once upon a time there was nothing. But if that were true there would be nothing even now, because something that does not exist can only be brought into being by something already existing. If nothing was in being nothing could be brought into being, and nothing would be in being now, which contradicts observation. Not everything therefore is the sort of thing that needs not be; some things must be, and these may or may not owe this necessity to something else. But just as a series of causes must have a stop, so also a series of things which must be. One is forced to suppose something which must be, and owes this to nothing outside itself; indeed it itself is the cause that other things must be. This is God. [22]

Something cannot come from nothing. Something can only come from something.

Elementary particles make up matter. Matter is made up of chemicals, chemicals are made up of molecules, molecules are made up of atoms, and atoms are made up of protons, electrons, neutrons, and quarks. When and if we ever get to the smallest elementary particle in the universe, the question will arise: What sustains it in existence?

Either this foundational particle always existed as the building block of all existing things, or God, existence itself, is the source and sustainer of all that exists.

Human experience teaches us that things that exist have a source for their existence. This is an innate sense, and such innate senses are never wrong. Thus, the existence of "things," even the most elementary particle, favors the existence of God over his non-existence.

An Aside

Any building block—even one that is postulated to have always existed, even prior to time—would have no consciousness and no life. Where would it get this life, this consciousness? (See the origin of life and consciousness questions.)

Scholastic philosophy argues that all things that exist do so because of *existence itself*. This subsistent existence gives existence, sustains it, and while being independent to what it sustains, gives it its life and consciousness.

"Things" are material. Existence itself is beyond the merely material.

6
CONSCIOUSNESS

Nature consists of a finite number of elements. Our human bodies consist of those elements. The elements themselves which we consist of, and nature itself consists of, have no consciousness—for elements do not have consciousness. If the elements of the universe do not have consciousness, and we are made up of such elements, why do we have consciousness? How does non-living matter become alive, become living matter?

> Science's biggest mystery is the nature of consciousness. It is not that we possess bad or imperfect theories of human awareness; we simply have no such theories at all. About all we know about consciousness is that it has something to do with the head, rather than the foot. [23]
> —Nick Herbert, Physicist

> Nowhere in the laws of physics or in the laws of the derivative sciences, chemistry and biology, is there any reference to consciousness . . . . This is not to affirm that consciousness does not emerge in the evolutionary process, but merely to state that its emergence is not reconcilable with the natural laws as at present understood. [24]
> —John Eccles, Neuroscientist

> No single brain area is active when we are conscious and idle when we are not. Nor does a specific level of activity in neurons signify that we are conscious. Nor is there a chemistry in neurons that always indicates consciousness. [25]
> —Mario Beauregard, Neuroscientist

> Despite centuries of modern philosophical and scientific research into the nature of the mind, at present there is no technology that can detect the presence or absence of any kind of consciousness, for scientists do not even know what exactly is to be measured. Strictly speaking, at present there is no scientific evidence even for the existence of consciousness. [26] [Consciousness is an immaterial phenomenon].
> —Allan Wallace, Philosopher of Science

Many attempts have been made to explain consciousness. Some scientists and neurologists have speculated about consciousness in terms of patterns of electromagnetic activation, brain wave sequences, brain wave collapses, synaptic tunnels, synaptic passages, neural networks, neural excitations, neurotransmitters, quantum waves, quantum discontinuities, and quantum cytoskeletal states. Others have promoted the belief that consciousness comes from the interaction of bosons and fermions, biological oscillators and bioplasma charged particles. Still others have tried to explain consciousness by the trajectory of particles, subtle energies, the excitation of condensates, and the working in unison of molecules. All forms of electro-chemical processes have been postulated.[27] All have failed. No scientific explanation has been able to explain consciousness.

At the heart of the problem is the nature of matter: I am matter. I am conscious. How can matter, which has no consciousness, be put together to produce consciousness? To make the point more concrete, the renowned scientist Roy Varghese gives the following explanation:

> Once you understand the nature of matter, of mass-energy, you realize that, by its very nature, it could never become 'aware,' never 'think,' never say 'I.' But the atheist position is that, at some point in the history of the universe, the impossible and the inconceivable took place. Undifferentiated matter (here we include energy), at some point, became 'alive,' then conscious, then conceptually proficient, then an 'I.' Matter . . . has none of the properties of being conscious and, given infinite time, it cannot 'acquire' such properties.[28]

Another problem deals with evolution. Random, chance evolution cannot explain the complexity of consciousness. The brain contains approximately 100 billion cells. Each cell is allied by synapses to as many as 100,000 other cells. If the brain could not have evolved without divine assistance within 3.7 billion years, if a single cell could not have evolved without divine assistance within 3.7 billion years, consciousness certainly could not have evolved without divine assistance within 3.7 billion years.

The odds favor God's divine intervention or design.

Another issue is whether consciousness is limited to the confines of the brain, and therefore completely naturalistic. For the famed scientist, Marco Biagini, this is not possible:

> Where does consciousness come from? The phenomenon of consciousness proves that, at a certain time, our psyche certainly began to exist in us. The problem with the issue of consciousness is that the laws of physics prove that consciousness cannot be the product of simply or solely physical, chemical or biological processes. Therefore, the origin of our consciousness is transcendent to physical reality.[29]
> —Marco Biagini, Ph.D., Solid State Physics

Is consciousness only within the brain, or does it, as Dr. Marco explains, transcend the limits of the brain. Are there experiences of consciousness that cannot be self-produced, that cannot be explained by a brain-alone, materialistic, atheistic theory? How do we explain the following claimed human experiences? Are these things possible? If even one of the below phenomena is possible, what are the implications?

- Out of Body—the ability to acquire new knowledge while being clinically dead.

- Déjà vu—the sensation or feeling that one has already experienced something that appears to be happening for the first time.
- Eureka Experience—a sudden understanding of what was previously incomprehensible.
- Precognition—the procurement of future information that could not be deduced from presently available, acquired sense-based data.
- Retrocognition—knowledge of the past which could not have been learned or inferred by normal means.
- Premonition—a strong feeling that something is about to occur.
- Intuition—an ability to know something without evidence.
- Telepathy—the transmission of information from one person to another through the use of the mind only.
- Remote Viewing—the ability to acquire knowledge of something that is hidden from view and separated by distance.
- Bilocation—when a person appears to be located in two distinct places at the same instance in time.
- Providence—the sense that things are not coincidental or chance occurrences.
- Prophetic Utterances—insights and predictions into future events.
- Free Will—to choose a course of action that is not pre-determined.

If any one of these above experiences are possible, then what are the implications that follow? The fact that these experiences are reported as happening throughout the world and throughout history makes one wonder.

If any one of the listed experiences of consciousness has a transcendental dimension, then we have entered into the realm of the divine.

It can be argued that consciousness is a participation in existence itself. If consciousness is a participation in existence itself, subsistent existence, then consciousness is not bound by the limits of space and time. Only participation in existence itself can make the above list—or part of the list—of supernatural phenomena possible.

The mystery and nature of consciousness, and our experience of conscious life, favors the existence of God over his non-existence. [30]

7
AQUINAS' ARGUMENT FROM NATURAL LAW

[Another argument for the existence of God] is based on the guidedness of nature. Goal-directed behavior is observed in all bodies obeying natural laws, even when they lack awareness. Their behavior hardly ever varies and practically always turns out well, showing that they truly tend to goals and do not merely hit them by accident. But nothing lacking awareness can tend to a goal except it be directed by someone with awareness and understanding . . . . Everything in nature, therefore, is directed to its goal by someone with understanding, and this we call God. [31]
—Aquinas

Let us examine an arrow flying toward a target. An arrow cannot hit its target without a bow propelling it. A bow needs an archer to propel it. An archer has awareness of what his goal is—hitting the target. If he did not have an awareness of what he was doing or an awareness of his goal, he would not be able to hit the target.

It is like a clock that is wound up. It takes an intelligent being, an aware being to wind up the clock, otherwise the clock will not begin to take time.

The sciences like math, physics, astronomy, chemistry, biology etc., are directed by laws and by goals. These laws of nature are meant to understand why things do the things they do. The whole scientific method presupposes laws, goals, and/or ends. Without these laws we would be blind to nature. Nature would be unpredictable and chaotic.

Either the natural laws of nature are directed or so ordered by that which has no awareness, like a clock without someone to wind it, or an arrow without an archer to direct it to its target, or the laws are directed by an intelligent or aware being that winds the clock and shoots the arrow with purpose.

The guidedness of nature favors God. Human experience favors the existence of God.

Everyone who is seriously engaged in the pursuit of science becomes convinced that the laws of nature manifest the existence of a spirit vastly superior to that of men, and one in the face of which we with our modest powers must feel humble. [32]
—Einstein

8
INTELLIGENT DESIGN[33]

When we look upon our world we observe order and design. If this were not so, there would be no laws of nature to study, no scientific method, and therefore no science. The very fact that we can observe disorder is because disorder is a deviation from order. We know a person with terminal cancer will die because we know that the cancer has disordered the design of the natural way a body is supposed to operate. We know all sickness because we can distinguish order from disorder, design from a damage to the design.

Order and/or design is either a product of chance or a product of intelligence. Everything in our experience of life that has order has an orderer, and everything in our experience of life that has design has a designer. Furthermore, with every passing decade, with every passing new horizon of knowledge, the sciences show us more, not less order, more, not less design!

Order and design in the universe favors the existence of an orderer to the order, a designer to the design. And this orderer, designer must be that which is beyond the limits of order and design. This is what we call God.

An Aside I

The very notion of chance implies order. In other words, how do you know chance unless you know order? You can only argue for chance if you know there is order. To say something occurred by chance is to say that something occurred in a way that was not expected! How can you expect something without order or design? How can you expect going home from work unless that is the order or the design of your day? That is, after work I go home. Ironically, if you argued that there is no order but only chance, then that world of only chance occurrences would be an order, a design, predictable.

An Aside II

What about disteleology? What about supposedly badly designed materialistic configurations we find in the universe? Many atheists point to body parts such as the appendix, the birth canal, the testes, the clitoris, the eye, the third eyelid, the sinus, the pharynx, the breathing reflex, the tonsils, wisdom teeth, the spinal column, goose bumps, hair, defective genes (i.e., GULO), and so forth, as proofs that the universe is not finely tuned. Other examples are found in other animal life forms (ostrich wings, panda thumbs) and in the universe (storms, earthquakes).

The very fact that we are able to identify supposedly poorly designed "things" presupposes order, design, and fine tuning. How can I know there is something contrary to order, unless there is an order? How can I know there is something contrary to design, unless there is a design? How can I know there is something contrary to a finely tuned universe, if there is no finely tuned universe?

With the advances in the sciences, we are learning that supposedly useless or vestigial "parts" are in fact quite necessary. Tonsils, the appendix, redundant veins, the location of the retina, the pineal gland, the spleen, the coccyx, the male nipple, wisdom teeth, hair, eyebrows, eye lashes, the ear muscle, the arrector pili, the thymus, and many more once thought of useless and poorly designed parts are no longer seen as such. Time and again, these allegedly useless or poorly designed parts have been shown to be quite valuable. The same can be said of other animal forms-ostriches using wings for stability in locomotion—and of the universe in general.

And if there are useless vestiges or imperfections, the evolution from unfit to fit, or imperfect to perfect, or more perfect etc., implies an orderly process, a design—as would an evolving universe.

9
INTELLIGENT DESIGN—THE CELL'S EVOLUTION

The cell is that which reads DNA and translates it into the structures necessary for life. But why does it read this DNA and why does it translate it into structures? What gives it its dynamism? Why must it be anything other than a pile of chemicals and forces just sitting there or moving around aimlessly? What gives it its drive, its purpose, its end? What makes a cell, building material, ordered by a blueprint, DNA, build?

The odds of a cell developing by chance, the odds of DNA developing by chance, the odds of a cell cooperating with DNA by chance is statistically impossible according to scientists and statisticians (1.6 followed by 59 zeros to one).[34]

There is no scientifically solid explanation for the existence of the cell. And when we add the dilemma regarding the origin of life, we are even more perplexed. In the words of the renowned cell biologist, Franklin Howard, "[There] are no detailed Darwinian accounts of the evolution of any biochemical or cellular system, only a variety of wishful speculations."[35]

Alternative explanations are needed. The Nobel Prize winning scientist Francis Crick, the atheist co-discoverer of the structure of DNA, had trouble dealing with the statistics involved with the birth of the cell. It is for this reason that he argued for a version of the panspermia thesis which argues that intelligent aliens seeded the earth with life. In his own words, "A spaceship from another planet brought spores to seed the earth."[36] Even the atheist Crick had to concede to an intelligent cause or being for life on earth. But this begs the question: "Who created these aliens?"

Others have been less extreme and have argued that meteors or fragments of astral collisions impregnated with the seeds of life brought life to earth. But who "impregnated" these meteors and fragments with the seeds of life? Where did these seeds of life come from?

Francis Crick rejects these and similar views because, according to his thinking, the seeds of life would have been too fragile to survive on a flying asteroid or meteor. A spaceship, according to Crick, would have been needed to protect the seeds.

Carl Sagan believed that one day extraterrestrials would come to earth and explain the origin of the human cell and human life to us.

Many scientists hold by faith—since there is not a single shred of evidence for its support—that there are billions upon billions of worlds and universes. By proposing multi-world or multi-universe theories, the statistical probabilities associated with the birth of the cell becomes more palatable, albeit still statistically improbable.

Even if we stretch the scientifically plausible, we are still left with the problem: In the words of the former atheist, Antony Flew: "[Multi-universe] or not, we still have to come to terms with the origin of the laws of nature, and the only viable explanation here is the divine Mind."[37]

The various panspermia, seeded asteroid, seeded meteor, and multi-world-universe theories, or more appropriately unfounded beliefs, are purely theoretical and contrary to cosmological observation. In the words of the renowned researcher and writer on modern science, Greg Easterbrook: "The multi-universe idea rests on assumptions that would be laughed out of town if they came from a religious text."[38]

Atheists like to disparagingly refer to the "God of the gaps"; well, I suppose we can refer to some atheist scientists as referring to the "aliens of the gaps," a science gap filler, a science form of "limbo theory." Theists and atheists both use "gap-fillers."

Ironically, to the dismay of atheists, these above theories, if they turned out to be true, would argue more for an intelligent designer than an atheistic worldview! As the Jesuit physicist Robert Spitzer argues, "these theories, intended to explain an atheistic source for life on earth, do the exact opposite: These unfounded attempts at explaining life on earth are so complex and convoluted that they would require a God-designer! They violate Ockham's razor, the canon of parsimony," the belief that the simplest explanation is usually the best—*simplex sigillum veri.*[39]

The earth is a privileged planet, a planet where life, and complex life at that, exists. One would expect that in a universe as expansive as ours that life would be abundant, yet even a single cell cannot be found anywhere except on this privileged planet. What are the odds?

If life could be found on other planets or anywhere beyond this planet, nothing changes in terms of belief or non-belief in God. However, if no life can be found in the universe except on this privileged planet, God's existence, to use a basketball phrase, is "a slam dunk" reality.

All that we experience is either a product of chance or of design. The evidence, common sense, and logic favors design. Human experience teaches us that order is formed by an orderer and design is formed by a designer. Why would the orderly, finely tuned laws of nature necessary for life be the only "things" that would have no orderer, no designer behind them?

Probability favors God's existence over his non-existence (*simplex sigillum veri*) for the origin and creator of the cell.[40]

An Aside

As with the other examples of infinite regress arguments, the prime designer, the first designer without a designer, is subsistent existence. Subsistent existence, existence itself stops an infinite regress.

10
INTELLIGENT DESIGN — TUNED FOR LIFE

Einstein argued that the big bang should have brought about chaos rather than order. Yet the universe is anything but chaotic. As Einstein would continue to argue, "Since the world has all the features of design, it must therefore have an ultimate designer (human experience affirms this since everything in our world that we see design in has a designer for the design).

We live on a privileged planet, a planet uniquely and finely tuned and ordered for life.[41]

Things that are tuned or ordered are more a product of design than chance, coincidence or synchronicity. That which is tuned is so because it was tuned by a tuner, just like a piano player tunes a piano. What or who is this tuner of a universe and planet predisposed for life, if not God?

Let us look at some of these finely tuned features that make life possible on this planet.

- If the temperature that resulted from the initial big bang at the beginning of the universe was a trillionth of a degree colder or hotter, the carbon molecule, which is the foundation of all life, would never have developed.
- If the cosmic rays existing at the beginning of the universe were slightly different (different angle, time or intensity) the hemoglobin molecule, necessary for human life, could never have evolved.
- If the age of the universe were older than it is, no stable burning star-types in the right part of the galaxy would be around. If the universe were younger, there would be no stars. In both cases there would be no life.
- If the expansion rate of the universe were larger there would be no galaxies. If smaller, the universe would have collapsed.
- If the ratio of exotic matter mass to ordinary matter mass were larger, the universe would collapse. If smaller, there would be no existent galaxies.
- Protons are 1836 times larger than electrons. If they were a little bigger or smaller, human life would not be possible.
- If the ratio of electron to proton mass were larger or smaller, chemical bonding would be insufficient for the chemistry of life.
- If the ratio of neutron mass to proton mass were higher, the formation of life would be impossible. If the ratio were lower, the universe would be an amalgamation of black holes.
- If the mass of the neutrino were larger, galaxy clusters and galaxies would be too dense to exist. If smaller, galaxies would never have formed.
- If the number of protons to the number of electrons were larger or smaller, electromagnetism would dominate gravity, preventing galaxy, star, and planet formation.

- Protons, with their positive electrical charge, balance out electrons, with their negative electrical charge. If this was not so, life would not be possible.
- If the decay rate of protons were greater, life would not be able to survive the accompanying release of radiation. If smaller, the universe would not have enough matter for life.
- If the strong nuclear force constant were larger, there would be no hydrogen for life to form. If smaller, no elements heavier than hydrogen would form, and thus the formation of life would not be possible.
- If the weak nuclear force constant were larger, stars would convert too much matter into heavy elements, making life impossible. If smaller, stars would convert too little matter into heavy elements making life unattainable.
- If water did not exist on this planet in three states—ice, water, and gas—life could not exist.
- If the polarity of the water molecule were smaller or greater, life could not develop.
- If white dwarf binaries were too few in number, there would be an insufficient amount of fluorine for life. If too many, planetary orbits would be too unstable for life.
- If the size of the relativistic dilation factor were larger or smaller, certain chemical reactions necessary for life would not be operational.
- If there were not the right combination of gases in the universe (even a slight variation) life would not be sustainable. Either an extreme greenhouse effect or an atmosphere bombarded by cosmic radiation would result.
- If the rate of carbon to oxygen nuclear energy level ratio were larger, the universe would have an insufficient amount of oxygen for life. If smaller, the universe would have an insufficient amount of carbon for life.
- If supernovae eruptions were too close, or too frequent, or too late, radiation would exterminate life on earth. If too distant, too infrequent, or too soon, then the necessary heavy elements to produce planets would be missing.
- If the initial uniformity of radiation were more uniform, there would be no life. If less uniform, the universe would be made up of black holes and empty space. There would be no life.
- If the earth's magnetic field were weaker, our planet would be devastated by radiation. If the magnetic field were stronger, we would be devastated by electromagnetic storms.
- If the ratio of the electromagnetic force to the gravitational force constant were larger, the sun would be among the smallest stars, making stellar burning insufficient to support life. If smaller, the sun would be larger

than most stars, making the production of heavy elements inadequate for life.

- If the gravitational force in the universe were larger, stars would be too unstable for life. If smaller, the stars would be too cool for nuclear fusion, and therefore insufficient for the existence of life.
- A slight change in the orbits of the planets would impact our moon, and therefore impact our earth's gravity to such an extent that life would not be sustainable.
- If the moon were a different size, wild fluctuations in temperature would follow, tides would be impacted, the proper mixing of nutrients in the oceans would be inadequate, and life would be unsustainable. If the average distance between galaxies were larger, there would be an insufficient amount of matter to form stars. If smaller, the sun's orbit would be unstable, making life impossible.
- If we were much further from the sun in our solar system, the oceans would be ice, and life would not exist. If we were much closer, the oceans would be boiling or vaporizing.
- If the average distance between stars were larger, rocky planets could not form. If smaller, planetary orbits would be too unstable to sustain life.
- If the density of galaxy clusters were denser, the sun's orbit would be disrupted. If less dense, there would be a lack of necessary material for the formation of stars. Life would not be achievable.
- If the sun's rays were more red or more blue (as seen in the flames that come off of logs in a fireplace) photosynthesis, the mechanism that allows for most plants to exist, would cease and we would cease to exist as well.
- A smaller or larger sun would make the planet uninhabitable.
- If the velocity of light were faster, stars would be too luminous to support life on earth. If slower, stars would be insufficiently luminous to sustain life.
- We live in the right kind of galaxy. Elliptical galaxies do not have the necessary heavy elements necessary for life, and irregular galaxies are prone to supernova explosions. Our spiral galaxy is ideal for fostering life. Jupiter's size and gaseous nature protects the earth from comets; and Mars, being at the edge of the asteroid belt, protects the earth from incoming asteroids. [42]

Intelligent design makes possible the scientific method, physics, mathematics, and all the sciences. Without an implied order, or implied laws of nature, there would be nothing other than chaos! Evolution and the mystery of the universe are far more a product of a divine orderer, an intelligent designer, than simply chance. A finely-tuned-for-life universe is much more likely the work of an intelligent designer than anything else. Human experience affirms the need for a designer for a design, an orderer for an order, a lawmaker for a law, etc. This belief is innate to healthy individuals, and innate beliefs from healthy individuals correspond to reality.

When examining what is necessary for life on earth, God's existence is favored over his non-existence. The physicist Albert Einstein summarizes this well:

> Everyone who is seriously engaged in the pursuit of science becomes convinced that the laws of nature manifest the existence of a spirit vastly superior to that of men, and one in the face of which we with our modest powers must feel humble . . . . Whoever has undergone the intense experience of successful advances in the domain of science is moved by profound reverence for the rationality made manifest in existence . . . the grandeur of reason incarnate in existence . . . . The deeply emotional conviction of the presence of a superior reasoning power, which is revealed in the incomprehensible universe, forms my idea of God. [43]

If life exists on other planets, God's existence or non-existence is not impacted. However, if life, complex life, only exists on this planet in a universe of planets, and in a universe that should be teeming with life according to secular thought, atheism as a belief system becomes troublesome—for such a world is counterintuitive to atheist thought.

11

INTELLIGENT DESIGN—EXPLOSIVE BIOLOGICAL JUMPS

The survival of the fittest presupposes the arrival of the fit.
—Tacelli

If we have evolved for belief in God, and what has evolved is the fittest, what
does this say regarding the unbeliever, the atheist?
—Anonymous

The scientific principle of *natura non facit saltum* is one that is held by
many, particularly those in the study of evolution. The atheist Charles Darwin held to this principle fervently: "Nature makes no jumps; only God
does!" But is this the case?

What does the fossil record teach us?

Some 550 million years ago the fossil record was inhabited by single or
simple celled organisms such as algae and bacteria. As we approach the 530
million year time period, multi-cellular organisms such as sponges appear,
and then an explosion takes place, an explosion that takes place within a
geological instant, five to ten million years—often referred to as the Cam-
brian Explosion. Within this geological instant, we find an explosion of cells
as well as an explosion of genetic information within organisms. The geological record radically changes from simple celled (five or less) organisms to
organisms with fifty or more cell types. The first bodied animals appear:
insects, crustaceans, and chordates are found for the first time, organisms
with new structures and new functions.

Statisticians and philosophers of science have estimated the odds of such
an explosion or evolutionary jump as being 10 to the 150th to one--that is, 10
with 150 zeros behind it to one. The chances of a Chihuahua composing the
complete works of Dante and Shakespeare are more likely!

If the scientific cliché holds that "nature makes no jumps, and only God
does" then God is more likely the cause of this jump.

The jumps continue. Around four hundred million years ago, within a
fifty million year period, we have a vertebrate explosion. Most of all fish
groups appear, with no apparent ancestors or descendants, and with no apparent transitional or intermediate forms.

Around three hundred and fifty million years ago, within a fifty million
year span, we have an amphibian explosion, with no apparent ancestors or
descendants, with no apparent transitional or intermediate forms.

Jumps continue. Reptile and mammalian groups emerge in a so-called
geological instant.[44] If "nature makes no jumps, and only God does" then
God is more likely the cause of this jump.

According to strict Darwinian evolution, species evolve from lower forms to higher forms through "numerous, successive, slight modifications."[45] The fossil record, therefore, should be filled with transitional, intermediate forms. Every geological formation, every stratum, should be full of such links.

The case is quite the opposite; there is a troubling lack of transitional or intermediate links.

The fossil record is full of examples of microevolution, but the fossil record lacks irrefutable examples of macroevolution. As the atheist Harvard professor Stephen Gould explained:

> The extreme rarity of transitional forms in the fossil record persists as the trade secret of paleontology. The evolutionary trees that adorn our textbooks have data only at the tips and nodes of their branches; the rest is inference, however reasonable, not the evidence of fossils.[46]

Microbiologist Michael Denton explains the heart of the dilemma:

> [When we] consider the evolution of A into B through a number of mutational intermediaries, [the following problem occurs]: Each new advantageous mutation or innovation . . . must first occur, and then spread by interbreeding to all the members of the species and the rate at which this occurs, the substitution rate, depends on a number of factors, including mutation rate, generation time, and total population number. Unless the advantageous mutation rate, the substitution rate and the total number of advantageous mutations are known, then it is simply impossible to assess whether the transition A to B could have possibly occurred by natural selection.[47]

The new field of molecular biology and the new field of comparative biochemistry have also been a source of concern for biologists in terms of transitory or intermediary species. By studying the sequential arrangement of proteins, the differences of protein sequences in living species, one can determine the relatedness of species. To this very day, molecular biology has not been able to show, irrefutably, any evidence of transitory or intermediate species. As Michael Denton explains:

> Thousands of different sequences, protein and nucleic acid, have now been compared in hundreds of different species but never has any sequence been found to be in any sense the lineal descendant or ancestor of any other sequence . . . . Each class at a molecular level is unique, isolated and unlinked by intermediaries . . . . At a molecular level, no organism is 'ancestral' or 'primitive' or 'advanced' . . . .[48]

Whether one agrees with Denton or not, molecular biology has posed great problems for the idea that evolution takes place in a slow and random process.

The punctuated equilibrium theory comes to the rescue, comes to fill the gap.[49] Since there is a troubling lack or non-existence of transitional or intermediate fossils to explain the evolution of man, Darwinian or Neo-Darwinian evolution has been revised by many scientists. They have adopted the punctuated equilibrium theory.

Simply stated, the theory of punctuated equilibrium argues for periods of dormancy (*stasis*) in evolution followed by explosive changes marked by branching speciation (*cladogenesis*).

Can the theory of punctuated equilibrium explain these jumps? Possibly. Or is saltation with macro-mutations a possible answer? Possibly. What about the neutral or nearly neutral theories of molecular evolution? What about symbiogenesis? Is there yet a synthesis of theories awaiting to be made? Possibly. Can such a synthesis allow for God? Yes.[50] Can an atheist hypothesize a world without evolution? No! Evolution is essential for atheist belief!

Given the choices, and the lack of evidence to support the current theories of evolution, the facts favor a providential-God-blueprint, a God-programmer who programmed some type of evolutionary process. Whatever the theory, God is favored over chance, coincidence, or synchronicity at this time in history.

God is more likely than less likely the source, sustainer, and director of evolution.

An Aside

When there is uncertainty, there is room for speculation, there is room for alternative evolutionary theories and interpretations. World renowned scientists, who believe in evolution, such as William Bateson, Hugo de Vries, Richard Goldschmitdt, G. Ledyard Stebbins, Lynn Margulis, Carl Woese, Barbara McClintock, John Caims, Stephen Gould, David Raup, Steven Stanley, Peter Corning, Jan Smuts, Elisabet Sahtouris, James Shapiro, Massimo Pigliucci, Motoo Kimura, Eugene, Koonin, Hans Driesch, etc., have differing approaches to the traditional theory of evolution. They reject the strict fundamentalistic Darwinian approach to evolution—an approach the "new atheists" or more appropriately "fundamentalist atheists" are obsessed with. Given the limits to the human brain and its evolutionary future, God may very well be the only one who will be able to fill the gaps that human knowledge will never be able to grasp!

12
EITHER WAY—THE INTELLIGENCE DILEMMA

Let us assume that atheists are correct. The universe is without design, and therefore without a designer or intelligence. The universe is simply ruled by chance, coincidence or synchronicity—which has no intelligence.

The problem: Humans have intelligence! How can this be, if we accept the atheist vision of the world as having no intelligence—having only chance, coincidence or synchronicity ruling its existence?

Where does this human being, this intelligent being, get this intelligence? Blind chance? Coincidence? Synchronicity? But how can blind chance, coincidence, or synchronicity—which has no intelligence--produce design and intelligence, produce an intelligent human being?

Human experience teaches that intelligence comes from intelligence, and that design comes from an intelligent designer!

The atheist premise—that all is chance, coincidence or synchronicity--is contrary to human experience. Our universe has all the marks of order and design, and all that has order or design in our daily experiences has an orderer, a designer, an intelligence as its source. We as humans have all the marks of order, design, and intelligence and therefore all the marks of an intelligence, a mind, as the source for our order, design and intelligence. This is logically intuitive.

God's existence, therefore, is favored over his non-existence.

13
ARGUMENT FROM PROVIDENCE

Coincidence is God's way of remaining anonymous.
—Einstein

Each small task of everyday life is part of the total harmony of the universe.
—Therese of Lisieux

What is providence?

Providence is that place between absolute free will and absolute predestination.

Providence is the view that there are no chance occurrences, coincidences or synchronicities in life.

Divine providence is "the plan by which God orders things to their true end. . . . Although the plan itself and in all its detail is entirely the work of God, in its implementation God deploys the natural and free activity of many intermediary and secondary agents. Furthermore, even moral evils and physical defects, as permitted [not willed] by God, cannot obstruct the consummation of the divine plan."[51]

With a general, albeit superficial, knowledge of the nature of providence, let us examine an event within the 20th century that seems to be anything but chance, coincidence or synchronicity. Let us examine a snippet of what can be hypothesized as being a part of God's divine providential plan.

On May 13, 1917 three young peasant children, Lucia dos Santos, Francisco Marto and his sister Jacinta saw a vision of Mary, the Mother of Jesus. They were told that on October 13, 1917, a miracle that all would see would occur. On October 13, 1917, in the presence of an estimated crowd of 70,000 pilgrims, and in the presence of Communist newspaper writers, the following occurred.

The atheist, pro-government, anti-clerical Lisbon paper, *O Seculo*, described the incident:

> From the road, where the vehicles were parked and where hundreds of people who had not dared to brave the mud were congregated, one could see the immense multitude turn toward the sun, which appeared free from clouds and in its zenith. It looked like a plaque of dull silver, and it was possible to look at it without the least discomfort. It might have been an eclipse which was taking place. But at that moment a great shout went up, and one could hear the spectators nearest at hand shouting: 'A miracle! A miracle!' . . . . Before the astonished eyes of the crowd . . . the sun trembled, made sudden incredible movements outside all cosmic laws---the sun 'danced' according to the typical expression of the people. People then began to ask each other what they had seen. The great majority admitted to having seen the trembling and the dancing

of the sun; others swore that the sun whirled on itself like a giant Catherine wheel and that it lowered itself to the earth as if to burn it in its rays. [52]

In the October 17, 1917 edition of the Lisbon paper, *O Dia*, we read:

At one o'clock in the afternoon, midday by the sun, the rain stopped. The sky, pearly grey in color, illuminated the vast arid landscape with a strange light. The sun had a transparent gauzy veil so that the eyes could easily be fixed upon it. The grey mother-of-pearl tone turned into a sheet of silver which broke up as the clouds were torn apart and the silver sun, enveloped in the same gauzy grey light, was seen to whirl and turn in the circle of broken clouds. A cry went up from every mouth and people fell on their knees on the muddy ground . . . . The light turned a beautiful blue, as if it had come through the stained-glass windows of a cathedral, and spread itself over the people who knelt with outstretched hands. The blue faded slowly, and then the light seemed to pass through yellow glass. Yellow stains fell against white handkerchiefs, against the dark skirts of the women. They were repeated on the trees, on the stones and on the sierra. People wept and prayed with uncovered heads, in the presence of a miracle they had awaited. The seconds seemed like hours, so vivid were they. [53]

From twenty-five miles away, the atheist (or more appropriately former atheist) Alfonso Lopes Vieira commented: "On that day of October I was enchanted by a remarkable spectacle in the sky of a kind I had never seen before." A schoolteacher, Delfina Lopes, along with her students, saw the spectacle of the sun from the town of Alburita—again, some twenty-five miles away. Mass hallucinations, or any other attempt at explanation, is hard to fathom from twenty-five miles away, especially when one is not expecting any phenomenon.

The little children would reveal to the people the following baffling revelations:

a. The prediction of a Bolshevik Revolution.

b. The prediction that an anti-God movement would spread from Russia to infect many nations (atheism, communism).

c. The prediction of World War II (Provenance of written document predicting WW II is attested to 1935).

d. The prediction that World War II would be preceded by a sign in the sky. World War II was preceded by the celestial event of an aurora borealis. A month after the aurora borealis, Hitler was on the march.

e. The prediction that Russia would return to Christianity if the country was consecrated to Mary. Pope John Paul II consecrated Russia to Mary. The Soviet Union ceased to exist, and atheism is now dying out in Russia, being taken over by the revival of Orthodox Christianity and Eastern Catholicism.

f. Finally, the childhood death of Francisco and Jacinto was revealed by Mary. She told them they would "be taken up to heaven." The children told their mother and pilgrims this would be so. Lucia, the only survivor, would become a nun and die in her convent at the age of 97 in 2005.

How do we explain this? Chance, coincidence, synchronicity?

If the future can be known, then this known future presupposes providence and providence favors the existence of God. If history is directed toward a providential end, this plan for this end, this providential future is more likely premeditated by God rather than chance, coincidence or synchronicity. In fact, atheism cannot account for providence.

Finally, Fatima is arguably a miraculous experience. If anything is a miracle, then God exists!

Is your life simply a series of coincidences?[54]

14
ARGUMENT FROM MIRACLES

Those considered for sainthood by the Catholic Church go through a rigorous process of scrutiny. First, the life, works, and writings of the holy person must be studied and deemed as heroically virtuous. Once this process is complete, then one awaits confirmation of this heroic virtuousness by one, preferably two "miracles," one for beatification and one for sainthood. Sometimes the second miracle is bypassed.

The cause of sainthood is taken up by the Vatican Congregation for the Causes of Saints. In terms of "miracles," the medical commission of physicians and scientists never pronounce "a miracle," rather they pronounce that a "remedy" or "unexplainable" cure has occurred which is contrary to modern science's aptitude and the modern scientific literature.

Underlying the relationship between saints and miracles is the belief in the communion of saints. This is a doctrine that teaches that our relationships change, but remain. Just as we can ask a loved one to pray for us here on earth, we can ask him or her to pray for us in heaven, in the very presence of God.

There is a beautiful expression of this belief in the words of the late Colonel David Heinz who died in the Israeli War of 1948: "As I stand upon the seashore, a beautiful sailing ship is in my view. I watch and watch until the sea and sky meet, and then she is gone. Where? Gone from my sight, that is all! And just as she is gone from my sight, she becomes visible in the site of others on the other side of the world. That is what dying is all about." Relationships change but do not end.

As we examine the following documented cases, we must ask ourselves whether we are dealing with coincidence, synchronicity, chance or dealing with that which breaks the boundaries of determinism and thus allows for the reality of something beyond the natural world to intrude—that intrusion being more likely divine than not.[55]

Jacalyn Duffin's 2009 exhaustive study *Medical Miracles: Doctors, Saints, and Healing in the Modern World* by Oxford University Press is a detailed documentation of scientifically inexplicable phenomena attributed to the supposed intercession of saints between the 16th and 20th century. I encourage all to explore this text.

Let us sample some of the proposed curative powers attributed to saints and the blessed—particularly those known to most Americans:

Brother Andre Bessette of St. Joseph's Oratory, Montreal

During his lifetime, Andre healed an incalculable amount of pilgrims who visited St. Joseph's Oratory. As a child I remember being awed by the number of crutches, wheelchairs, braces, etc., that covered the walls of the oratory.

In his death, Brother Andre continued to bring healing. Joseph Audino, calling upon the intercession of Brother Andre, was cured of cancer in 1958.

Elizabeth Ann Seton

By calling upon Elizabeth Ann Seton, Anne Theresa O'Neill was cured in 1959 of acute lymphocytic leukemia. Carl Kalin was cured of fulminating rubeola meningo-encephalitis in 1963. Sister Gertrude Korzendorfer was cured of inoperable pancreatic cancer in 1935 through the intercession of Elizabeth Ann Seton.

John Neumann

Eleven year old Eva Benassi was cured on her deathbed of acute peritonitis. Michael Flannigan was diagnosed at the age of six with cancer and given six months to live. He was cured in 1963.

Frances Xavier Cabrini

Through her intercession, Peter Smith, blinded by an accident, recovered his sight in 1921.

Katherine Drexel

Her intercession is attributed to the healing of Amy Wall and Robert Gutherman in 1974. Both were cured of deafness.

Kateri Tekakwitha

Jake Finkbonner, an eleven year old Indian boy, was healed in 2006 of a flesh-eating bacteria.

Fulton Sheen

Travis and Bonnie Engstrom gave birth to a stillborn child on September 10, 2010. With no pulse for sixty-one minutes, the doctors proceeded to declare the child dead. Suddenly, baby James had a heartbeat. He is a healthy child, with no signs of brain damage—which is usually the case when a brain goes without oxygen for ten minutes.

Padre Pio—Stigmatist

Consiglia De Martino was healed in November of 1995 of a ruptured thoracic duct and a huge lump filled with lymphatic fluid. Chest x-rays and a CT scan confirmed the disappearance of any signs of illness. Matteo Pio Colella was healed in January of 2000 from septic shock, weak breathing, and an irregular heartbeat. After being revived by doctors after a cardiac arrest, he was placed on a respirator. He remained in a comatose stage. After his mother prayed at the tomb of Padre Pio, the boy recovered. He has no lingering effects.

John Paul II

The Costa Rican mother of four, Floribeth Mora Diaz, who had been diagnosed with an inoperable brain aneurism in 2011, sought the help of John Paul II. Confined to bed, with a one month prognosis of life, her prayers, she believes, were answered. Her aneurism disappeared. Dr. Alejandro Vargas Roman stated of his patient: "If I cannot explain it from a medical standpoint, something non-medical happened." Another miracle attributed to John Paul II is the healing of the French nun Sister Marie Simon-Pierre, who recovered from Parkinson's disease in 2005.

Sister Faustina Kowalska

Maureen Digan was healed of incurable lymphedema in March of 1981 after praying at the tomb of Sister Faustina.

John XXIII

In May of 1966 Sister Caterina Capitani was healed after calling upon John XXIII. After undergoing fourteen operations for gastric hemorrhages, doctors had little hope for her future recovery. She would recover completely.

Damien de Veuster (Leper of Molokai)

Sister Simplicia Hue was cured of "intestinal disease" in September of 1895. Audrey Toguchi was cured of cancer in 2008.

John Bosco

Sister Mary Joseph Massimi, after being given the last rites, and suffering from a duodenal ulcer was cured in 1928 by Bosco's intercession. Catherine Lanfranchi Pilenga, suffering from chronic arthritic diathesis and organic lesions, was restored to health in 1931.

Maximilian Kolbe

In July of 1948, through prayer to Kolbe, Angela Testoni was cured of intestinal tuberculosis. In August of 1950, Francis Rainer was cured of calcification of the arteries/sclerosis.

Joan of Arc

Therese Belin, suffering from peritoneal and pulmonary tuberculosis, complicated by an organic lesion of the mitral orifice, was cured in August of 1909. Others attributed to be healed through her intercession include Therese of Saint Augustine of leg ulcers, Julie Gauthier of cancer of the left breast, and Marie Sagnier of cancer of the stomach.

When we look to the late-twentieth century, the following "miracles" have been attested to as not explainable through science or current medical knowledge. Nine miracles have been attributed to the Cardiac System, four to the Vascular System, thirteen to the Respiratory System, twenty-eight to the Neurological System, twenty-eight to the Gastrointestinal System, nine to the Liver System, six to the Genitourinary System, ten to the Gynecological System, four to the Eye System, one to the Ear System, two to the Endocrine System, eight to the Bone and Joint System, and six to the Blood and Lymphatic System. Other miracles have been associated with the skin, wounds, infections, and tumors.[56]

When we look at the "unexplained phenomena" attributed as "cures" from the 16th century to the 20th century, we find 1,410 cases![57]

As we examine the documented cases, we must ask ourselves whether we are dealing with coincidence, synchronicity, chance or that which breaks the boundaries of determinism and thus allows the reality of something beyond the natural world to intrude—and if there is such an intrusion, this intrusion is more likely God than not?

An Aside

What about psychosomatic healing? Or spontaneous healing? All these are possible. But a stillborn child or infant would not seem to be subject to psychosomatic occurrences. Also, the healing of the ill by the prayers of others not associated with the ill, also eliminates the likelihood of psychosomatic healings. As far as spontaneous healing, this is possible, but not likely in so many cases (1,410 cases). Given the fact that people specially sought intercession from believed saints, does not make spontaneous healing likely.

Lourdes

One of the most famous places to find documented miracles is found in Lourdes, France where it is believed that Mary, the mother of Jesus, appeared to a young girl Bernadette.

Lourdes has a medical bureau with doctors of various religious persuasions, including atheist doctors. If a cure seems to have no medical reason behind it, the case is sent to the International Medical Committee of Lourdes—a committee of specialists. After examination, a pronouncement is made. The doctors never pronounce "a miracle," rather they make the pronouncement that the "cure" is "unexplainable" according to modern science and the modern scientific literature. Since 1905, with the establishment of the medical bureau, sixty-four inexplicable phenomena have been declared as "unexplainable" by modern science.

Henri Busque was cured on April 28, 1858 of tuberculosis, purulent adenitis, a septic ulcer, and inflamed lymph glands. Louis Bouriette was cured of blindness in his left eye on July 28, 1858. Justin Bouhort, unable to walk and suffering from consumption, was restored to complete health in July of 1858. Madelaine Rizan was cured on October 17, 1858 of a left-sided paralysis that kept her bedridden. Marie Moreau was restored to health on November 9, 1858 after suffering from blindness. Blaisette Cazenave was healed on January 18, 1862 of a chronic infection of the conjunctivae and eyelids. Aline Bruyere received her miracle on September 1, 1889, being cured of pulmonary tuberculosis. Joachime Dehant was cured on October 13, 1878 of a gangrenous ulcer on her right leg. Ameilie Chagnon was restored to health on August 21, 1891 after suffering from a long series of "bone diseases" and tuberculous arthritis. Clementine Trouve was healed of tuberculous osteoperiostitis of the right calcaneum on August 21, 1891. Elisa Lesage was cured of ankylosis of the joint in the right knee on August 21, 1892. Father Cirette was restored to health on August 31, 1893, being cured of a nervous disorder brought about by influenza. Aurelie Huprelle was healed of "cavitating pulmonary tuberculosis" on August 21, 1895. Esther Brachman regained her health on August 21, 1896 after suffering from tuberculosis. Jeanne Tulasne was healed of Pott's disease on September 8, 1897. Clementine Malot came to Lourdes with a case of "tuberculosis with spitting blood" and was cured on August 8, 1898. Rose Francois was restored to health on August 8, 1899 after a year of suffering from the effects of a "chronic infection of the right arm, with numerous fistulae and gross lymphoedema of the upper arm and forearm." The capuchin priest, Father Salvator was healed of tuberculous peritionitis on June 25, 1900. Marie Savoye was healed of rheumatic fever and heart disease (with signs of a mitral lesion) on September 20, 1901. Sister Hilaire was cured of chronic gastroenteritis on August 20, 1904. Sister Beatrix was cured of tuberculosis and laryngeal-bronchitis on August 31, 1904.

Marie-Therese Noblet was healed of Pott's disease "of peculiar appearance, owing to some concomitant nervous phenomena" on August 31, 1905. Cecile Doubille de Franssu was restored to health on September 21, 1905 after being cured of tuberculous peritonitis. Antonia Moulin suffered from an abscess of the right leg with phlebitis and lymphangitis; she was restored to health on August 8, 1907. Marie Borel was healed of abscesses, fistulas, and bowel obstructions on August 21, 1907. Sister Macimilien was restored to health after being cured of a hydatid cyst of the liver with phlebitis of the left leg on February 5, 1908. Virginie Haudebourg suffered from constant urinary infections, cystitis and nephritis. She was cured on May 17, 1908. Johanna Bezenac suffered from progressive cachexia, localized lesions, and a severe pneumonia when she was cured on July 2, 1908. Pierre de Rudder, on July 24, 1908, regained his ability to walk. Marie Mabille was cured of a "long-standing chronic infection in the right iliac fossa, with vesical and colonic fistulae" on August 8, 1908. Sister Marie of the Presentation was saved from starvation on August 15, 1908 after being cured of a case of "chronic gastroenteritis." Anne Jourdain was healed of "tuberculosis with gross apical lesions" on October 10, 1908. Elisa Seisson was made well on July 12, 1912, being healed of "chronic bronchitis with severe organic heart disease."

If there are things that cannot be explained or will ever be able to be explained on merely human grounds, then there are such realities as "miracles." And if there are truly miracles, then there is a God. [58]

Life's experiences favor the existence of miracles, and therefore favor the existence of God over his non-existence.

15
ARGUMENT FROM DEFICIENCY

The definition of science according to the Merriam-Webster dictionary is as follows: science is the "knowledge or a system of knowledge covering general truths or the operation of general laws especially as obtained and tested through."

The scientific method is described in the following manner: One begins with a hypothesis or conjecture to be tested. This presumes causes and effects, order, and laws. One must be able to test a hypothesis—which implies observations and evaluations. Finally, there is the conclusion (i.e., morning follows night).

In our day to day experiences every law has a lawmaker, every effect has a cause, and every order has a source of order, an orderer. If this is so within our daily experiences, why would it not apply to all dimensions of reality?

The human person is an orderly being. As the kids like to recite in the Dem Bones song, *"The toe bone's connected to the foot bone, The foot bone's connected to the ankle bone, The ankle bone's connected to the leg bone, The leg bone's connected to the knee bone . . . ."*

If our bodies are subject to the laws of nature and to order, then that which functions contrary to proper ordering, the proper functioning of the person, is lacking, impotent, deficient.

If our bodies are subject to the laws of nature and to order, then that which functions according to the proper ordering, the proper functioning of the person, is more complete, full, whole, and thorough.

That which is lacking is less likely than that which is fuller for comprehending the possibility of the existence of God.

Is atheist belief detrimental to the proper functioning of the human person? Or is belief in God?

Positive versus Negative Well-Being

God-believers have better mental and physical health and a better quality of life. The Mayo Clinic report of 350 studies regarding physical health and 850 studies regarding mental health found that God-centered religions and spiritualties brought about better health outcomes and quicker recovery times from ailments. [59] Stephen Joseph from the University of Warwick, after studying the relationship between belief in God and disbelief, found that believers are happier and healthier in every dimension of their lives. Such people who have had religious experiences score lower on psychopathology measures and higher on psychological well-being scales. [60]

In 2000 the Iona Institute reported, from its examination of forty-two studies involving approximately 126,000 subjects, that active God-believers tended to live longer than atheists by 29 percent, and that Church attending believers increased their chances of living longer by as much as 43 percent. [61]

The World Health Organization and the renowned sociologist Phil Zuckerman of Pitzer College have documented that the suicide rate among atheists far exceeds that of God-believers. When classifying nations according to beliefs, atheistic secular nations are marked by higher suicide rates, despite being among the richest of nations. Catholic countries have a suicide rate of 4 per 100,000; Protestant Countries have a rate of 13.8 per 100,000. Atheistic countries have a rate of 31.1 per 100,000. [62]

In a University of British Columbia study, secular schools, at all levels, were found to produce higher rates of mental illness and mild forms of functional impairment than religious schools. Children who were spiritual were happier than those who were not. Children who had strong personal and communal dimensions to their spirituality had a 27 percent higher rate of happiness and meaningfulness to their lives versus the non-spiritual. [63]

Atheists are half as likely to get married and more likely to have few or no children.

Seventy percent of atheists are male, and 38% of the males are between the ages of 18-29. [64]

Atheists Are Prone to Violence

From 1917 to 2007 approximately 148 million people were killed by atheist run countries (some estimates claim as much as 250 million). Atheistic states have a 58 percent greater chance of mass murdering their populations than any other group! [65]

The statesman Zbigniew Brzezinski wrote in his work Out of Control that "atheistic communism [was] the most costly experiment and failure in human history." [66]

The Nobel Prize winner Aleksandr Solzhenitsyn wrote:

> I have spent 50 years working on the history of the [communist] revolution. In the process I have read hundreds of books, collected hundreds of personal testimonies, and have contributed eight volumes of my own toward the effort of clearing away the rubble left by that upheaval. But if I were asked today to formulate as concisely as possible the main cause of the ruinous revolution that swallowed up some 60 million of our people, I could not put it more accurately than to repeat: 'Men have forgotten God; that's why all this has happened.' [67]

In terms of religious wars, when one examines the *Encyclopedia of Wars* by Charles Philips one observes that of all the wars in recorded history, only 123 of them can be attributed to religion. That is seven percent of all the wars in history. If we eliminated Islam from the mix, war in the name of religion would account for only three percent of all wars. When we look to just the twentieth century, atheistic regimes have killed three times more people in war than any other group.[68]

Most wars are caused by the desire for power, honor, money, fame, territory, and other worldly desires. They are caused by secular motives.

If belief in the divine is an advantage to well-being and survival since time immemorial, what are the possible implications for such truths? Could atheism be the consequence of some yet unknown abnormality, detrimental mutation or underdevelopment?

An Aside—Modern Atheist Atrocities

The French Revolution—with its atheist "cult of reason"—forced 20,000 priests to resign under the threat of death or imprisonment. Thirty thousand priests were forced to leave France and those who refused were executed by guillotine or deportation to French Guiana. France's 40,000 churches were either closed, sold, destroyed, or converted for secular uses. To this day, France has never recovered from the French Revolution's Reign of Terror!

Under Germany's Secular-Atheist Liberal Movement of 1871–1878, half of the Prussian bishops were imprisoned or exiled, a quarter of the parishes lost their priests, half of the monks and nuns were exiled or fled persecution, a third of the monasteries and convents were closed, and 1800 parish priests were imprisoned or exiled. Thousands of lay-persons were imprisoned for helping priests.

The atheists Nietzsche and Schopenhauer formed the very foundation and structural framework for Hitler's Nazi Germany. Hitler personally gave a copy of the writings of Nietzsche to Stalin and Mussolini. Hitler abolished religious services in schools, confiscated Church property, circulated anti-religious and anti-Catholic material to his soldiers, and closed theological institutions. The Nazi government closed down Catholic publications, dissolved Catholic youth leagues and charged thousands of priests, nuns and lay Catholics with false crimes. Church kindergartens were closed, crucifixes were removed from schools, Catholic presses were shut down, and Catholic welfare organizations were banned. Thousands of Catholic lay persons and clergymen and nuns were arrested and sent to Nazi concentration camps. Over 300 monasteries and institutions were confiscated by the SS. More than 2,600 priests were killed in Nazi concentration camps. The Dachau Concentration Camp had a dedicated barrack for priests.

The militant atheistic Soviet Union through mass executions, warfare, imposed starvation and forced labor destroyed millions upon millions of individuals. They confiscated churches and made them into museums of atheism—the Leningrad Kazan Cathedral became the Museum of the History of Religion and Atheism. Leon Trotsky's regime killed twenty-eight bishops and 1,200 priests. Statistics point to the fact that six to eight million people were killed under Lenin, twenty to twenty-five under Stalin—including 50,000 priests. Eastern Europe, under Soviet rule, accounts for at least two to three million deaths in the name of communism. From 1917 to 1969 the Soviets destroyed 41,000 of 48,000 churches. Before the communist revolution there were 66,140 priests. On the eve of WWII there were only 6,376.

Mao's China equals in terms of carnage that of the Soviet Union.

In Tibet 7,000 temples and monasteries were destroyed; in North Korea 440 of 500 Buddhist temples were demolished; and in Vietnam 240 of 700 Buddhist temples were dismantled. *Jane's Intelligence Review* of October 20, 2000 explains that 168 of 273 suicide bombings between 1980 and 2000 were done by Marxist atheists—the Liberation Tigers of Tamil Eelam being among the most prolific of bombers.

The Spanish (atheist) Red Terror of 1936 killed 6,832 priests, 2,265 members of Catholic religious institutes, and 283 nuns. Between 1930 and 1936 the Jesuit religious order was dissolved, Church property was confiscated, religion was prohibited from being taught, and 58 churches were burned to the ground.

Mexico's atheist reign of terror led by the "Red Shirts" and the Radical Socialist Party between 1926 and 1934 led to the expulsion and assassination of over 4,000 priests. In 1926 there were approximately 4,500 priests in Mexico; in 1934 there were only 334.

From 1917 to 2007 approximately 148 million people were killed by atheist run countries (some estimates claim as much as 250 million people). In fact, atheistic states have a 58 percent greater chance of mass murdering their populations than any other group!

The belief in that which transcends oneself is the only cause that can keep a person and a culture from disintegrating—for the belief in that which transcends oneself is the only thing that can keep one answerable to something other than oneself or one's fellow man![69]

What about the Neurological Dimension to Belief versus Disbelief?

The renowned neuroscientist Mario Beauregard explains that the brain is too complex to simply identify God-belief with a single area. The well accepted neuroplasticity of the brain makes the simplistic, robotic, static, fixed, predetermined model of life and the brain too simplistic for suitable advanced research. As Mario Beauregard affirms through his work with functional magnetic resonance imaging (fMRI), "Complex cognitive and emotional processes have been shown to be mediated by neural networks compromising several brain regions, so it is very unlikely that there is a 'God' part in the brain responsible for spiritual cognitions, sensations, and behaviors."[70]

Given that the majority of the brain is active during spiritual experiences (particularly mystical episodes), and given that there are areas of the brain that are dormant or less active in non-spiritual, atheistic experiences of life, what are the implications for the spiritual and non-spiritual?

In a recent study at Boston College regarding the correlation between atheism and high functioning autistics, the following was observed:

> It is hypothesized that traits typically displayed among high functioning autistic individuals such as attraction to scientism and hyper rationality . . . render . . . individuals less likely to embrace supernaturalism and religious belief. Consistent with this, atheism and agnosticism are more frequent in the high functioning autistic groups . . . . Previous research has established systemizing and low conformity as prominent traits among HFA individuals. We propose that HFA individuals would be likely to construct their own belief systems, drawing on their interest in systemizing and lack of need to conform to approved social behaviors. [71]

People with high functioning autism are people with a neural developmental disorder characterized by impaired social interaction. It affects information processing in the brain by altering how nerve cells and their synapses comment and organize. Recent studies seem to indicate that those with high functioning autism are predisposed towards atheism because of the mind's inability to grasp supernatural concepts. For at least some, we must say that atheism has biological or more specifically neurological roots. If this is so for some, can it be possible for others? Could categorical and militant atheism be a neural developmental disorder? Could there possibly be an Atheist Personality Disorder?

Recent brain studies are beginning to shed light on belief and non-belief. The neural picture of the brain is being mapped more than ever. Differences are already being seen. Some studies have shown that God-believers have more brain tissue in their frontal lobes than some atheists. This area of the brain is associated with attention and reward. Some atheists seem to have larger hippocampi than some God-believers. This area of the brain is associated with memory and emotions—a possible reason behind the psychological and sociological predispositions for both groups. Some God-believers have higher levels of dopamine in their system, which is associated with increased attention and motivation. This could be a possible reason why atheists suffer higher rates of depression, suicide, anger and "sloppy thinking." [72]

Studies are pointing more and more to biological and even evolutionary reasons for religious belief and disbelief. In a series of tests held by the University of Toronto Department of Psychology, researchers found significant differences in how God-believers and atheists responded to stress. The authors of the test wrote: "These results suggest that religious conviction provides a framework for understanding and acting within one's environment, thereby acting as a buffer against anxiety and minimizing the experience of error." The God-believers' anterior cingulate cortexes operate differently than that of most atheists. This area is associated with stress and anxiety. God-believers seem to be predisposed to calmness under stress and in the face of the unknown.[73] Belief in God seems to be a genetically programed advantage for the survival and well-being of the human species. It may be for this reason that atheists suffer higher rates of mental and psychological disorders.

Secular societies that do not believe in God or are led by people who do not believe in God are worse off than societies that believe in God. God-belief is healthier for cultures, societies, and nations.

There are many more examples why atheists are possibly deficient or disorderly or functioning improperly. Some of the other causes for atheism are attributed to the dysfunctional father, mother, and family, the narcissistic urge for recognition or non-conforming, a pathological response to social disintegration, a hedonistic predilection for personal convenience and self-centeredness, and the inability to understand suffering. Still other causes for atheism are attributed to malnutrition at childbirth, abnormal brain development, and extreme maternal anxiety—resulting in the detrimental release of hormones. Post-traumatic stress from abortion—often referred to as Post Abortion Trauma—which leads to an inability to bond with prospective spouses and children, has also been correlated to a predisposition for atheism.

At the heart of all atheism is the inability to bond—thus the anti-social nature of atheists.

What is said of the individual, can also be said of society in many ways.

Deficiency in the Spiritual, Excess in the Sensual[74]

If there is no spiritual, there is only the sensual that is left. Without the spiritual, self-centeredness, hedonism, and an obsession with the *self* reigns. As seen from the above neurological studies, this may be due to a dysfunction or an underdeveloped brain, as regards the spiritual dimension of the person.

Michel Onfray, a proud proponent of hedonism, finds justification for his lifestyle in atheism.

Freud was a cocaine user who was euthanized by his doctor Max Schur in 1939. It is remarkable that in a survey of 4000 British doctors, atheist or agnostic doctors were twice as likely to favor euthanizing the ill.[75]

Margaret Sanger, Planned Parenthood's icon, was known for promoting birth control, abortion, and eugenics. She was renowned for favoring open marriages and sexual promiscuity. What was Margaret Sanger's objective?

"[Our objective is] unlimited sexual gratification without the burden of unwanted children . . . . The most merciful thing that the large family does to one of its infant members is to kill it."[76]

Madalyn Murray O'Hair had many lovers and believed that any form of sex between consenting adults was acceptable.

The Marquis de Sade's obsession with sadism, with sexual debauchery, was so intense that he would deny God and the morals of his time in order to satisfy his limitless sexual desires. He also endorsed abortions to eliminate unwanted pregnancies.

Bertrand Russell was known for his many affairs. Disingenuously, he expressed distress when one of his wives committed adultery.

Jean Paul Sartre had an "open relationship" with Simone de Beauvoir. He often took on her female sexual cast-offs. Sartre was notorious for his escapades with his female students.

Simone had many sexual affairs with men and women. Simone lost her teaching license for her inappropriate behavior with her students.

Karl Marx was notoriously lecherous, exploitive of friends, unfaithful to his wife, and sired an illegitimate son.

Schopenhauer acquired syphilis as a result of his promiscuity and believed in what he called tetragamy—the marriage of two men to one woman.

Many atheists are well-known for practicing polyamory—one man dating and having sex with several women and one woman dating and having sex with several men.[77]

Nietzsche became insane near the end of his life, likely caused by syphilis. Sigmund Freud and Carl Jung explained that Nietzsche caught syphilis in a homosexual brothel in Genoa, Italy.[78] Nietzsche was sympathetic to pederasty—sex with adolescents—although there is no proof that he engaged in such activity.[79]

Some hedonistic atheists are advocates of pederasty. They are leading founders, advocates and supporters of organizations like NAMBLA—the North American Man-Boy Love Association.[80]

A disproportionate amount of the A disproportionate amount of the so-called LGBT (Lesbian, Gay, Bisexual, Transgender) community are atheists. Atheism insulates them from their lifestyle choices.

The pornography industry is made up of practical, categorical and militant atheists.

When there is no God to answer to, life becomes, in the words of Nietzsche, "brutish."

> If God is dead then everything is permitted.[81]
> —Dostoevsky, Russian Novelist

Conclusion

God-belief is justly, correctly, and rightly understood as an advantage and a superior mode of human existence than non-belief. If belief in the existence of God is beneficial for survival and well-being, and if atheism is marked by psychological and sociological abnormalities, then what can one infer apropos the God-believer and the atheist sociologically, psychologically, neurologically and biologically?

In our day to day experiences every law has a lawmaker, every effect has a cause, and every order has a source of order, an orderer. If this is so within our daily experiences, why would it cease in other dimensions of reality?

The human person is an orderly being. If belief in God is detrimental to the well-being and function of the human person, then belief in God is likely contrary to the laws of nature and order. If belief in God is beneficial to the well-being and function of the human person, then belief in God is in agreement with the laws of nature and order.

If our bodies are subject to the laws of nature and to order, then that which functions contrary to proper ordering, the proper functioning of the person, is lacking, impotent, deficient. If our bodies are subject to the laws of nature and to order, then that which functions according to the proper ordering, the proper functioning of the person, is more complete, full, whole, and thorough.

If disbelief in God is detrimental or even a personality disorder, then God's existence is favored over his non-existence, for that which is deficient is less apt to know or recognize reality than that which is healthier, functionally stable or more stable. A healthy human nature favors the existence of God over his non-existence, for that which works or functions properly is more dependable in accessing reality than that which works or functions ineffectively, inadequately or in a distorted manner.

If atheism is a disorder, as science could argue, then atheism is less likely to have a realistic grasp on reality.

On the other hand, it is clear that the healthy innately believe in God. Hence, the healthy are more likely to have a grasp on reality.

Therefore God's existence is favored over his non-existence because belief in God is found in the healthy who naturally have a better grasp on reality.

An Aside

What makes the human person superior to the lower animals? Spirituality. Spirituality is only found in human beings. Belief in God only exists in human beings. What does this imply regarding those who deny, reject, or fail to develop their spiritual being (and the spiritual dimension of the brain)?

Lower animals, who have no spiritual nature, are by nature atheistic. Those who deny, reject, or fail to develop their spiritual nature, are relegated to the level of the lower animals, lower atheistic animals. Atheism is not an elevation in one's human nature, but a diminishing in one's human nature—a diminishment to a lower form of animal life.

Argument from Universal Consent

If we have evolved for belief in God, and what has evolved is the fittest, what does this say regarding the unbeliever, the atheist? Healthy human beings have always believed in the existence of God. The likelihood of healthy humans being wrong is less likely than unhealthy beings.

16
ARGUMENT FROM BONDING AND SELF-REFLECTION
(AN ARGUMENT FROM DEFICIENCY)

Why is atheism an overly male phenomena (70%)? Is it possible that the upbringing of atheists is responsible for their atheism? Scientists from Freud to the modern psychologist Paul Vitz seem to think so. Is it possible that atheists have a disproportionate inability to bond, and if so, does their inability to bond with family, friends, and society, have detrimental results in bonding with a possible God? Is it possible that atheists repress self-reflection which is necessary for belief in or recognition of God? Let us examine a cross-section of famous atheists of the modern era. [82]

- Nietzsche's father died before he was five. Reflecting upon the death of his father he wrote: "Transfixed by the idea of being separated for ever from my beloved father, I wept bitterly . . . . I will never forget the gloomy melody of the hymn 'Jesus my faith.'"[83] Nietzsche viewed his mother and women in general as inferior. Men were for war and women were for recreation. Women, for Nietzsche, were no better than cats and birds, or "at best, cows."[84] In his insane years, Nietzsche would refer to himself as the "anti-Christ."[85]
- David Hume's father, Joseph, died when he was two, leaving him with a sense of bitterness and anger.
- Bertrand Russell's father, Lord Amberly, died when Bertrand was four. His grandfather, a possible father substitute, died when he was six. Russell fought bouts of suicidal thoughts throughout his childhood and adolescence. Bertrand Russell lost his mother at the tender age of two.
- Jean Paul Sartre's father, Jean Baptiste, died when Sartre was fifteen months old. Jean Paul was left with his grandparents. Sartre viewed his grandparents as old, weak, and manipulative. Jean Paul Sartre's mother, after the death of her first husband, remarried a man who openly rejected Jean Paul. Sartre's mother, after the remarriage, became distant and abandoned him to his aloof grandparents.
- Albert Camus' father, Lucien, died when Albert was one. He would find no adequate substitute father figure.
- Arthur Schopenhauer's father, Floris, committed suicide when Arthur was seventeen. Arthur Schopenhauer's mother was distant and uncaring. Schopenhauer was the product of an unwanted pregnancy. Schopenhauer blamed his mother for his father's suicide.
- Albert Ellis's mother was distant and unaffectionate. While hospitalized for nearly a year as a result of a childhood illness, his mother rarely visited him.

- Jean Meslier, although a priest, was secretly an atheist. Jean was forced into the priesthood and into celibacy by his father. After Meslier's death, his atheism came to light through his anti-clerical, pro and pre-French Revolution writings. As he would write of himself, "I was never a believer."
- Voltaire, a deist or practical atheist, was anti-Church and anti-clerical. He was an admirer of Jean Meslier. When he was seven years old his mother died, and his father sent him away for schooling. Suspecting that he was an illegitimate child, he changed his name from Arouet to Voltaire, thereby disavowing his family heritage. Voltaire's mother was an absent figure and was viewed by Voltaire as promiscuous.
- Jean d'Alembert's father died when he was twelve. He would find no adequate substitute father figure.
- Ludwig Feuerbach viewed his father as impulsive and volatile. His father Anselm abandoned his family at the age of nine. Anselm moved in with his mistress Nannette Brunner. He would only return to his wife and son upon the death of his mistress.
- Samuel Butler was often beaten by his father in childhood. In adulthood, father and son publicly expressed their mutual hate for each other.
- Sigmund Freud referred to his father as a sexual pervert and as a weak man—passive in his response to anti-Semitism. Freud's hatred for his father is powerfully depicted in a childhood dream: the young Sigmund urinates on his father's bed.
- Joseph Stalin and his mother received severe beatings from Joseph's alcoholic father.
- Mao Zedong viewed his father as a tyrant.
- Russell Baker's father died when he was five. He recalls having intense tantrums of rage against God. [86]
- Karl Marx viewed his father as bourgeois and saw him as a weak man who converted to Christianity for superficial reasons, for social and political advancement.
- Richard Carlile's father was an alcoholic and died when Richard was four.
- Madalyn Murray O'Hair, who is responsible for the banning of prayer in public schools in the United States, hated her father with a passion. She once took a knife and threatened to kill him. In her words, "I'll see you dead. I'll get you yet. I'll walk on your grave." [87]
- Kate Millet was abandoned by her father at the age of thirteen. Her father ran off with a nineteen year old girl. Kate would express her disappointment by declaring that she would never allow a man to become important in her life. [88]
- Jill Johnston was deceived by her mother and abandoned by her father. It was later found that Jill's parents were never married. Jill's mother would

call her daughter a "bastard" and in turn she would call her mother a "whore."[89]

- Antony Flew, the atheistic psychologist and philosopher of science was caught after having too much to drink, lying on the floor crying out over and over again, "I hate my father. I hate my father."[90]

Is it possible that atheists have a hindered ability to bond and if so, does their inability to bond with family, friends, and society have detrimental consequences for bonding with a possible God? (Paul Vitz's classical work "Faith of the Fatherless" seems to indicate so.) Does their upbringing repress the desire for self-reflection which is necessary for belief in God? How can one pray "Our Father," if one's father is a poor or absent figure? How can one love God, when one has never experienced the nurturing love of a mother?

The atheist lifestyle is more likely than less likely a deficient form of life, and arguably a disorder.

Believers are more fully human, less lacking, more functionally perfect, and therefore capable of comprehending reality more effectively, completely—as it truly is. A healthy human nature is more dependable in accessing reality than one that is disordered.

Belief in God is integral to healthy human natures. A healthy human nature favors the existence of God over his non-existence, for that which works or functions properly is more dependable than that which works or functions ineffectively, inadequately or in distorted manner.

To reiterate: If atheism is a disorder or a defective way of life, as science seems to be moving towards, then atheism is less likely to have a realistic grasp on reality.

On the other hand, it is clear that the healthy innately believe in God. Hence, the healthy are more likely to have a grasp on reality.

Therefore God's existence is favored over his non-existence because belief in God is found in the healthy who naturally have a better grasp on reality.

The social sciences and a healthy human nature favor the existence of God over his non-existence.[91]

An Aside

The neuroscientist Richard Davidson published research indicating that meditative people have better coordinated neural networks than those who do not meditate—thus giving those who meditate a heightened sense of self-awareness—One is less likely to believe in God, a profound interior notion, if one has a poor awareness of the self![92]

Argument from Universal Consent

If we have evolved for belief in God, and what has evolved is the fittest, what does this say regarding the unbeliever, the atheist? Healthy human beings have always believed in the existence of God. The likelihood of healthy humans being wrong is less likely than unhealthy beings!

17
ID, EGO, SUPEREGO—ARGUMENT FOR GOD
(AN ARGUMENT FROM DEFICIENCY)

Traditional psychology often describes the human person in terms of the Id, Ego, and Superego. While Freud has fallen into disfavor over the years, this dimension of Freud's thinking still holds sway among most. [93]

Id

The Id is a term used to describe a human's innate, instinctual drive for pleasure and immediate gratification. It is marked by need, desire, urge, compulsion, libido and aggression. The Id is only concerned with self-gratification. Uncontrolled it would lead to debauchery.

Superego

The Superego is marked by the internalization or introjection of attitudes and norms of behavior, especially those instilled by parents, educators, or admired role models. The Superego has often been referred to as an "inner critic," or "conscience." It is engaged in fostering socially appropriate responses to internal and external realities. When the Superego is infected by extremes, repression or capitulation, the Superego can have negative consequences (i.e., inappropriate guilt feelings, depression, obsessions. anxiety, inferiority, compulsivity, and so forth).

Ego

The Ego is often referred to as the "reality principle" of the "I." It is where self-mastery takes place. It is where reason and common sense is active. It is directed to modulation, direction, and regulation. It is focused on the harmonious functioning of the Id with the Superego.

The Ego is equipped with defense mechanisms that help balance the tension between the Id and the Superego. Some of the common defense mechanisms include denial, displacement, repression, suppression, sublimation, introjection, projection, rationalization, dissociation, idealization, regression, etc. Depending on the mechanism used by the Ego, negative or positive consequences can follow. Thus the need for a healthy Ego.

Without a guiding principle, extrinsic to the self, and informative to the self, the Id, Superego, and Ego are subject to "disordered development." For example, an unhealthy Ego leads to debauchery or hedonism (i.e., the Marquis De Sade), which ultimately leads to emptiness, depression, and psychological pathologies of all kinds. If the Superego is unhealthy, then one is subject to similar psychological disorders often due to inappropriately internalized or introjected attitudes and norms of behavior, especially those in-stilled by deficient parents, educators, or poor role models (i.e., Vitz's deficient Father figure and its correlation to atheism). The Ego is called upon to serve as an "arbitrar" between the Id and Superego. If the Ego is not healthy, the arbitration functions poorly.

Given the above, where do we find people that we admire for living life authentically, marked with qualities such as prudence, temperance, justice, fortitude, wisdom, courage, modesty, goodness, joy, peace, patience, charity, humility, mildness, generosity, etc.? Looking at the last 2000 years of history, we can definitely exclude atheists, since they are characteristically angry, intolerant, vengeful, and deceptive (If you have any doubts about the psychological studies that affirm such affirmations, visit atheist websites, or read the twits of followers of atheists: Your doubts will quickly fade away. Hell hath no fury like that of an atheist!). So where can we find the most human of people with the best of the virtues discussed above—the Saints! Why?

Grace is the answer. What is grace? God. The giver is the gift. And if grace, God is not the answer, then there is something that saints have access to that makes them superior beings, authentically human beings. For our purposes, we will call this reality grace.

Grace heals, elevates, and builds upon human nature. In a sense, it heals, elevates, and builds upon the Ego so that the Ego functions the way it is ideally meant to function. It is grace that makes the possibility of being fully human a reality. Grace allows the Ego to function as it is meant to function. It reinforces, supports and energizes the Ego to function properly, humanly, authentically.

Grace, by healing, elevating and building upon nature, upon the Ego, allows for the most appropriate, reasonable and healthy functioning and balancing of the Id, the instinctual drives, and the Superego, the conforming drives, in such a way that life is lived out most fully, abundantly, and healthily—in a fully human manner.

Without responding to grace, to God, this living in a fully human manner functionally becomes virtually impossible or at best highly diminished. Again, let us resort to the example of atheists. The vast majority of atheists come from broken homes, lacking appropriate parental figures—as innumerable sociological studies have shown. Parental values—part of the Superego—are thus absent or gravely diminished. This inevitably leads to the Id having a disproportionate impact. Many "new atheists" make no apologies for seeking to create a "philosophy of hedonism." Many of the "old atheists," such as the Marquis de Sade, likewise made no excuses. Without grace, the Id can often overwhelm the Ego, the "I." On the other hand, the Superego, without the influence of grace, can overwhelm, in a negative manner, the Ego. We will stay with our example of the militant atheist. Instead of sublimating the hurt inflicted by non-existent or abusive parental figures in a positive manner, the defense mechanism of repression is often used, which often leads to the anger and confrontational spirit that is almost universally associated with militant atheists.

Grace, another word for God, is operative on the Id, Ego, and Superego.

The Ego arbitrates between the Id and the Superego. Grace heals, elevates and builds upon the Ego, allowing the Ego to function at its most appropriate manner. It is grace that allows the Ego to form a person into an authentically, properly, fully human.

Grace, another name for God, for the "giver is the gift," empowers authentic self-mastery, wisdom, the proper modulation, directing and regulating of the Id, Ego, and Superego. It allows for the proper mechanisms which permits the best possible and harmonious functioning of the Id, Ego, and Superego.

Since without God, without grace, being fully or authentically human is virtually impossible, and since the Saints most beautifully exemplify humanness lived to its fullness (As the cliché goes: "There are no gloomy saints."), then what can we infer from this reality?

In our day to day experiences every law has a lawmaker, every effect has a cause, and every order has a source of order, an orderer. If this is so with our daily experiences, why would it cease in other dimensions of reality?

If God, as existence itself, as one that eliminates an infinite regress of designers, is the Prime Designer, then one that best functions to its design is more likely to know reality and live reality the way it is meant to be lived, without delusion or distortions of reality. Given the example of the saints, given the examples of atheists, the Ego, as the "arbitrar" between the Id and Superego, functions most effectively in God-believers than non-God-believers, by virtue of the testimony of their lives.

Design favors a Designer, and God is the Prime Designer by virtue of being existence itself, subsistent existence. God—thus eliminating an infinite regress of "designers." Those who believe in God live happier and more virtuous lives—as exemplified by the saints. Those who live in an unhappier manner and in a less virtuous manner lack this belief—as exemplified by atheists.

Thus, God's existence is favored over his non-existence, for design is favored over chaos. That which functions most properly is more true to reality. Humans function most properly to the extent and level that they are God-believing beings.

God-belief, and God's probable existence, is more in line with reality, and the perception of reality—the psychologically healthy recognize reality better than the psychologically deficient or ill.

Argument from Universal Consent

If we have evolved for belief in God, and what has evolved is the fittest, what does this say regarding the unbeliever, the atheist? Healthy human beings have always believed in the existence of God. The likelihood of healthy humans being wrong is less likely than unhealthy beings!

18
STUNTED PSYCHOSEXUAL DEVELOPMENT ARGUMENT
(AN ARGUMENT FROM DEFICIENCY)

A kindergarten concept of God or the academic sciences is very much different from a college-level concept of God and the academic sciences. Often people go to college with at best an eighth grade understanding of God, and yet have a high school or above understanding of the academic sciences and arts, and of almost everything else. And then we wonder why people lose their faith in college. They are still stuck in their eighth grade or kindergarten concept of God.

If we look at the psychological development of persons, we find similarities to the above analogy. If we do not nourish our being, if we do not foster psychological growth, similar consequences follow.

If a person has not moved, psychologically, beyond a childhood concept of God, then that person is likely to have great difficulties believing in God in his or her adult years. Anything that stunts a person's psychological and/or spiritual development will either lead to a distorted spirituality or no spirituality at all.

Pre-Puberty

Prior to puberty a child is predisposed to immanentism, egocentricism, narcissism, or self-centeredness. Healthy childhood development is marked by an expanded vision of reality where concepts of transcendence, self-giving and other-centeredness develops—qualities essential for belief in God. If a child has not progressed during this stage of development, in this pre-puberty stage, this childhood stage, then the child will enter into adolescence and likely adulthood with an inability to grasp the possibility of God, since the possibility of belief in God requires a sense of transcendence, self-giving and other-ness. Atheism, studies have shown, is characterized by egocentrism, immanentism, and many argue narcissism—in fact, many psychologists argue that atheism is a narcissist-related disorder. If one does not develop psychologically and properly through childhood into adolescence then the likelihood of atheism is more probable. [94]

Adolescence

Adolescence is a time for developing one's moral standards and values as one's own, as opposed to that of one's parents, or society's. It is a time where there is a battle between the Id, moral laxity, and the Superego, hyperrigidity. Unresolved issues in this stage of development can lead to a surrendering to the Id and the abandonment of parental and societal norms in morals and values (i.e., a rejection of religion and God). Alternatively, failure to develop the Ego during this stage can lead to a Superego that predisposes one to fundamentalism, which taints one's entire life—either in the form of fundamentalist atheism or fundamentalist theism. It is a vision of the world that is oversimplified, a vision that is superficial and safe, but repressive.

Adolescence is characterized by individualism versus dependence, rebelliousness versus conformity, alienation versus dependence. It is a time where one is developing as an individual, as an autonomous person distinct from one's parents. This phase of development leads to the stage of adulthood where one personalizes, perfects, revises, and synthesizes the world in such a way that one becomes a healthy individual with a sense of purpose and meaning and a sense of solidarity and other-centeredness. If one does not progress into adulthood, or is stunted during this adolescent stage, then one is likely to reject in the name of individualism, alienation, and rebelliousness one's parental as well as society's—a parental alternative—norms, values, and spirituality. Atheists are known for their rebelliousness, narcissism or hyper-individualism (i.e., a love for being seen as "freethinkers," and "brights" and their opponents as "simpletons").

Belief in God or disbelief in God is more a psychological-biological phenomenon than an intellectual phenomenon. A healthy development from childhood to adulthood leads to belief in God. A stunted or unhealthy or poorly developed growth pattern predisposes one to atheism. Even the atheist Freud affirmed this reality. The question: How does this reality favor the existence of God?

God-belief is justly, correctly, and rightly understood as an advantage and a superior mode of human existence than non-belief. If belief in the existence of God is beneficial for survival and well-being, and if atheism is marked by psychological and sociological abnormalities, then what can one infer apropos the God-believer and the atheist sociologically, psychologically, neurologically and biologically?

In our day to day experiences every law has a lawmaker, every effect has a cause, and every order has a source of order, an orderer. If this is so within our daily experiences, why would it cease in other dimensions of reality?

The human person is an orderly being. If belief in God is detrimental to the well-being and function of the human person, then belief in God is likely contrary to the laws of nature and order. If belief in God is beneficial to the well-being and function of the human person, then belief in God is in agreement with the laws of nature and order.

If our bodies are subject to the laws of nature and to order, then that which functions contrary to proper ordering, the proper functioning of the person, is lacking, impotent, deficient. If our bodies are subject to the laws of nature and to order, then that which functions according to the proper ordering, the proper functioning of the person, is more complete, full, whole, and thorough.

If disbelief in God is detrimental or possibly a personality disorder, then God's existence is favored over his non-existence, for that which is deficient is less apt to know or recognize reality than that which is healthier, functionally stable or more stable. A healthy human nature favors the existence of God over his non-existence, for that which works or functions properly is more dependable in accessing reality than that which works or functions ineffectively, inadequately or in a distorted manner.

If atheism is a disorder, as science is showing more and more, then atheism is less likely to have a realistic grasp on reality.

On the other hand, it is clear that the healthy innately believe in God. Hence, the healthy are more likely to have a grasp on reality.

Therefore God's existence is favored over his non-existence because belief in God is found in the healthy who naturally have a better grasp on reality.

An Aside I

It worth noting that psychologists have found that adolescence has been—in many people in our modern era—extended into a person's twenties and thirties. It is therefore not coincidental that, given the above development, that people return to their faith in this modern era in their late thirties and forties.

An Aside II

For Freud—because of his negative view of the role of "illusion" in childhood and adolescence development—religious belief was seen as contrary to or a distortion of reality. Modern psychoanalysis has shown quite the opposite. Proper psychological development requires religiosity. It is religious belief which nourishes and directs healthy human development. It is religious belief that fosters creativity, spontaneity and imagination, which creates, shapes, and transforms life with a sense of purpose and meaning and a sense of self and destiny.

An Aside III

One's psycho-sexual development—which implies the healthy development of self-organization, self-integration, self-realization, self-determination, self-cohesiveness, and personal identity—if stunted, can predispose one towards atheism. Part of one's sexual identity is the ability to transcend the self into the other, to transcend oneself into the other. Without a developed sense of transcendence, one is not likely to have the ability to experience the transcendence of God. Stunted psycho-sexual development, among the various narcissistic pathologies associated with it, also impacts one's ability to believe in God.

Argument from Universal Consent

If we have evolved for belief in God, and what has evolved is the fittest, what does this say regarding the unbeliever, the atheist? Healthy human beings have always believed in the existence of God. The likelihood of healthy humans being wrong is less likely than unhealthy beings!

19
STUNTED PSYCHOSOCIAL DEVELOPMENT ARGUMENT
(AN ARGUMENT FROM DEFICIENCY)

Besides biological development, to perceive reality authentically presupposes the complete, harmonious, and healthy development and completion of the Id, Ego, and Superego, and the complete, harmonious and healthy development of the psychosexual and psychosocial phases of life.[95] Freud was preoccupied with the psychosexual stages of development, Erikson would built upon Freud and develop the psychosocial stages of development.

Infancy

It is in infancy that an infant learns to develop a sense of trust or mistrust. This is done primarily through the infant's relationship with his or her family, and in particular with his or her mother.

A mother's or father's love, protection, concern, and dependability fosters an ability to trust oneself and others. It enables the ability to depend on others and to entrust oneself to others in self-confidence.

Those who do not develop properly in infancy often grow to mistrust and lack confidence in others. Belief in God requires an act of trust, an act of self-surrender, an act of receptivity in hope—for belief in God implies a leap into the uncontrollable unknown.

Without trust or hope, one becomes stunted in an infantile understanding of reality, and a distorted one at that—where life is lived with mistrust and often hopelessness. The atheist personality type is marked by mistrust and at times hopelessness: "Trust no one! Question everything! This is all there is!" Or as Nietzsche would say, "Life is brutish." Or in the words of the Novelist, Dostoevsky, "If God is dead, anything is permitted." Or in the words of Albert Camus: "There is only one seriously philosophical question, and that is suicide." Hopelessness can predominate.

One who has not developed properly in the infancy stage of trust vs. mistrust, will at the very least have a distorted vision of reality, and at worst, an atheist personality.

Early Childhood

Early childhood development is characterized by the development of a sense of autonomy. Failure to develop properly leads to a personality marked by doubt.

As a child in a family one begins—because of a sense of safety, a sense of trust—to assert and express oneself, to develop self-control, self-esteem, and an ability to cooperate with others, who are recognized and respected in their autonomy. The failure to develop this basic sense of autonomy, leads to self-doubt, low self-esteem, and a lack of self-confidence. Paul Vitz, Ph.D., pioneer in the field of the psychology of atheism would identify this sense of self-doubt, etc., with the "sophistication urge" associated with atheist personalities.

Doubt, whether self-doubt, or doubt in general, predisposes one to disbelief.

Belief in God requires humility—to know oneself authentically—rather than low self-esteem. Belief in God requires a good sense of self and others, and a willingness, in confidence and trust, to be open to internal reorganization and development. This is the mark of the saints.

One who has not developed properly in the childhood stage of autonomy vs. doubt will at the very least have a distorted vision of reality, and at worst, an atheist personality.

Play and School Age

The play and school age stages of development are characterized by either initiative or guilt, industry or inferiority. These development stages take place in the family, the extended family, and the pseudo-family, the school.

These stages where initiative and industry (productivity) are affirmed leads to a sense of conscience, responsibility, dependability, self-discipline, diligence, perseverance, cooperation, and maturity. A community of faith would not function without these qualities. Atheists tend to be anti-social, at least according to the current prevailing studies.

On the other hand, a failure to develop in these stages is marked by guilt, inferiority, a rigidity in thought and often a self-punishing inferiority complex. Explore the internet and see how many times atheists like to reference IQ tests and ignore social competency tests. Search the internet and see how often they berate their opponents with insults rather than facts or arguments (In the words of the atheist philosopher, Julian Baggini, "Atheists need an enemy to give them their identity.") Explore the internet and see how often you can identify an atheist by their urge for sophistication—Vitz's "sophistication urge" theory.

One who has not developed properly in the childhood stages will at the very least have a distorted vision of reality, and at worst, an atheist personality.

Adolescence

The adolescence stage is characterized by the development of a healthy sense of identity or unhealthy identity diffusion—a proper lack of self-identity

(Nietzsche, in his later years, called himself "superman," the "anti-Christ," and the "Crucified One").

Healthy development is marked by self-awareness, self-acceptance, self-knowledge, and the awareness of others, and thus a healthy understanding of communal living.

Signs that one did not properly progress through this stage is exemplified by a personality that is prone to selfishness, self-centeredness, and narcissism.

Belief in God is primarily, albeit not necessarily, a communal experience. It requires the acceptance of the self in order to trust in confidence, in order to transcend the self into the ultimate other in a communal, interpersonal manner. Atheists, lacking this trust and confidence, are prone to self-centeredness (atheists are among the least charitable in terms of time and treasure donations, according to current statistics).

One who has not developed properly in the adolescence stage, will at the very least have a distorted vision of reality, and at worst, an atheist personality.

Young Adulthood

Young adulthood is characterized by the development of intimacy versus isolation. This is a stage of development where one learns to relate intimately and meaningfully in mutual reciprocity. It is marked by fulfilling relationships. The failure to develop in this stage predisposes one to personal isolation and an incapacity to establish intimate and mutually reciprocal relationships. The capacity for empathy is often missing.

Atheists have a higher rate of divorce, are disproportionately pro-abortion, and have a tendency toward anti-social behavior. Life for many atheists is meaningless. In the words of Richard Dawkins, "There is no design, no purpose, no evil and no good, nothing but blind pitiless indifference."

One who has not developed properly in the young adulthood stage will at the very least have a distorted vision of reality, and at worst, an atheist personality.

Adulthood

Adulthood is characterized by generativity versus self-absorption. A person who develops well in this phase of development is usually gifted with creativity in interacting with others cooperatively and an ability to be other-centered, without a desire for being recompensed. One develops an ability to be unselfish and self-sacrificing. Those who fail to develop, become self-absorbed, self-indulgent, self-loving, selfish, and even narcissistic.

Camille Paglia, an atheist, recognizes the role of spirituality as a necessary and driving force in art and life. "Art is a religious experience . . . .The spiritual quest marks all great art . . . [Artists] are spiritual seekers." Atheists, for Camille Paglia, have a "stunted imagination" incapable of bringing to art what art exemplifies, the transcendent, the mystical, the spiritual. God-believers are spirit-led, spiritual seekers. [96]

One who has not developed properly in the adulthood stage will at the very least have a distorted vision of reality, and at worst, an atheist personality.

Maturity

Maturity is characterized by integrity versus despair or self-contempt. Maturity is accomplished when all the previous stages of development have been successfully developed. To the extent that one has reached maturity, it is to that extent that one has reached a healthy acceptance and proper integration of the Ego, the self, life, and one's destiny. Those who do not reach maturity end up prone to despair, self-contempt, meaninglessness, and despair. In the words of Betrand Russell, "Life is purposeless and void of meaning." Or in the words of Richard Dawkins, "There is no design, no purpose, no evil and no good, nothing but blind pitiless indifference."

The end of life for many famous atheists echoes despair: Voltaire cried, "I have been abandoned by all . . . I shall go into nothingness." Severus whispered, "I have been everything and everything is nothing!" Thomas Paine explained, "I would give worlds if I had them . . . . I am at the edge of hell all alone." Carlile sniveled, "I am as good as without hope, a sad old man gazing into the final chasm." Sir Thomas Scott sobbed "Until this moment, I thought there was neither God nor hell . . . " Edward Gibbon despaired, "All is dark and doubtful." Sir Francis Newport cried, "All is over, all is lost." Hobbes said, "I am about to take a fearful leap into the dark . . . ." Marx shouted to his nurse, "Get out, get out. Let me die alone." Taleran admitted, "I am suffering the pangs of the damned." Vollney cried incessantly "My God, My God, My God . . . " Meravue exclaimed, "Give me opium that I may not think of eternity."Aldamont summarized it best, "Life was hell, and there is another hell ahead." [97]

One who has not developed properly into maturity will at the very least have a distorted vision of reality, and at worst, an atheist personality.

God-belief is justly, correctly, and rightly understood as an advantage and a superior mode of human existence than non-belief. If belief in the existence of God is beneficial for survival and well-being, and if atheism is marked by psychological and sociological abnormalities, then what can one infer apropos the God-believer and the atheist sociologically, psychologically, neurologically and biologically?

Let me reiterate what was previously said: In our day to day experiences every law has a lawmaker, every effect has a cause, and every order has a source of order, an orderer. If this is so within our daily experiences, why would it cease in other dimensions of reality?

The human person is an orderly being. If belief in God is detrimental to the well-being and function of the human person, then belief in God is likely contrary to the laws of nature and order. If belief in God is beneficial to the well-being and function of the human person, then belief in God is in agreement with the laws of nature and order.

If our bodies are subject to the laws of nature and to order, then that which functions contrary to proper ordering, the proper functioning of the person, is lacking, impotent, deficient. If our bodies are subject to the laws of nature and to order, then that which functions according to the proper ordering, the proper functioning of the person, is more complete, full, whole, and thorough.

If disbelief in God is detrimental or even a personality disorder, then God's existence is favored over his non-existence, for that which is deficient is less apt to know or recognize reality than that which is healthier, functionally stable or more stable. A healthy human nature favors the existence of God over his non-existence, for that which works or functions properly is more dependable in accessing reality than that which works or functions ineffectively, inadequately or in a distorted manner.

If atheism is a disorder or a deficiency, as science seems to be reflecting, then atheism is less likely to have a realistic grasp on reality.

On the other hand, it is clear that the healthy innately believe in God. Hence, the healthy are more likely to have a grasp on reality.

Therefore God's existence is favored over his non-existence because belief in God is found in the healthy who naturally have a better grasp on reality.

An Aside I: Paul Vitz's Sophistication Urge Theory

Low self-esteem or an inferiority complex is often expressed in the desire for being recognized. Low self-esteem is a characteristic trait found in atheists. Turning to atheism gives some people a sense of purpose and meaning, of being recognized, of being superior. Atheists often like to be seen as unique and sophisticated, as freethinkers and "brights," as rebels and new atheists. It gives them their sense of identity.

Paul Vitz explains: "Voltaire's ambition and intellectual vanity are agreed upon by all his biographers. His passion was for fame . . ."

Feuerbach has been described as a lonely figure whose loneliness "was the product of an unsatisfied intellectual vanity." He saw himself as a "philosopher of outstanding importance."

Nietzsche's pride and arrogance are widely acknowledged. Indeed, his philosophy is a celebration of this reality. His obsession with power, with being a "superman," with "killing God" exemplifies this inherent need for recognition. Nietzsche supplanted Christ with himself. He often referred to himself as "the Crucified One"—hardly a sign of modesty. In his insane years, he called himself the "Anti-Christ." Nietzsche sought to shock by denigrating the dignity of women, and by attacking Christian virtues and Christianity in general. He wanted to shake up the world by bringing upon it "a universal madness" by killing God. Ironically, in his attempt to destroy God, and bring the world madness, Nietzsche destroyed himself and brought upon himself madness![98]

Albert Camus loved to shock, as when he said, "There is only one seriously philosophical question, and that is suicide."[99]

An Aside II

Piaget, Kohlberg, and Fowler, building upon Freud and Erikson, have developed a psychology of faith. What has been said from all the previous psychological arguments is also pertinent and valid for the psychology of faith. It is hard to study psychological development and not find in the atheist some kind of personality deficiency. Disorder is associated with an unrealistic vision of the world and reality. God-believers, and particularly the saints, are marked by authentic and full humanness, and thus, a true perception of reality—and in their reality God exists.

In your free time explore the stages of Piaget's eras and stages of logical and cognitive development, and Kohlberg's six morals stages. Stage six is most insightfully developed by Meissner, S.J., in Life and Faith, Georgetown University Press.

An Aside III

In a recent study at Boston College regarding the correlation between atheism and high functioning autistics, the following was observed:

> It is hypothesized that traits typically displayed among high functioning autistic individuals such as attraction to scientism and hyper rationality . . . render . . . individuals less likely to embrace supernaturalism and religious belief. Consistent with this, atheism and agnosticism are more frequent in the high functioning autistic groups . . . . . Previous research has established systemizing and low conformity as prominent traits among HFA individuals. We propose that HFA individuals would be likely to construct their own belief systems, drawing on their interest in systemizing and lack of need to conform to approved social behaviors.[100]

People with high functioning autism are people with a neural developmental disorder characterized by impaired social interaction. It affects information processing in the brain by altering how nerve cells and their synapses comment and organize. Recent studies seem to indicate that those with high functioning autism are predisposed towards atheism because of the mind's inability to grasp supernatural concepts. For at least some, we must say that atheism has biological or more specifically neurological roots. If this is so for some, can it be possible for others? Could categorical and militant atheism be a neural developmental disorder? If so, reality is less likely to be perceivable in a defective brain.

It is interesting to note that high functioning autistic adults have a lot in common with atheists: poor communication and interpersonal skills, an inability to experience empathy and make lasting friendships, an inability to see the perspective of others, and an obsession with certain topics and the "here and now."[101]

Argument from Universal Consent

If we have evolved for belief in God, and what has evolved is the fittest, what does this say regarding the unbeliever, the atheist? Healthy human beings have always believed in the existence of God. The likelihood of healthy humans being wrong is less likely than unhealthy beings!

20

ARGUMENT FROM COMFORT

The devil's greatest weapon is not convincing us there is no God, but that we
have plenty of time.
—C.S. Lewis, Oxford Scholar and Novelist

There is an account of three demons preparing to depart for earth with the
intention of corrupting the souls of as many people as possible.

Before their departure to earth the demons each met for a final briefing
with the chief of demons, Satan. Satan asked the first demon, "How do you
plan on corrupting souls?" The first demon responded, "I plan to convince
people that there is no God." Satan then turned to the second demon and
asked, "What do you plan?" I plan" he responded, "to convince people there
is no hell." Satan seemed well pleased. Then he addressed the third demon,
"And what about you?" The third demon responded, "I'm simply going to
tell people that there is plenty of time to prepare for death and that the second
coming of Jesus is far away." Satan giggled and jumped with joy in front of
the third demon and said with great enthusiasm, "Do that my child and you
will corrupt many!"

Advances in the health sciences, improved hygienic living conditions and
nutrition have led to improved health and longer life span potentials. This
corresponding improved quality and length of life has dulled the need for
God. When death is on one's mind, questions involving one's destiny—
eternal or not—come to the fore. As the question of death and personal
suffering and quality of life is less significant so too is the need for God.

Taking into account numerous variables (i.e. plaques, wars, climate, civil-
ity) associated with the determination of life expectancy, the following general ages are associated with the following epochs:

- Pre-Neo-Paleolithic, 13
- Neo-Paleolithic, 18
- Classical Rome and Greece, 28
- 1200–1300, 43
- 1300–1400, 34
- 1400–1500, 48
- 1500–1550, 50
- 1600, 35
- 1700–1800, 25–40
- 1900, 48
- 2000, 77
- 2010, 78

The longer one lives the more one is focused on the here and now, the secular, the materialistic, the atheistic. Living to 13 makes one quite conscious of death and one's eternal destiny. When one lives to 90 then one can put off thoughts of death and one's eternal destiny.

Living longer and healthier can often put off reflections on the truly important aspects of life. It is no coincidence that the teenage, college, and early work years tend to be marked with little spirituality and Church attendance. One becomes overly preoccupied with the "things" of life and predisposed to think of oneself as indestructible. As one becomes settled in one's career, older, more cognizant of the reality of death, then one is more likely to ask the important questions of life: "What is life all about? Is there any purpose or meaning to life? Am I just a biological being that lives and dies, or is there something more? What does all this around me mean? Why is there life rather than no life? Why is there a world, rather than no world? Why is there existence, rather than no existence? Why?" In these reflections, one recognizes that life without God is a farce! One recognizes that the only sufficient answers to such questions cannot be answered by the "here and now."

The hunger for meaning and purpose, and all the core questions of life find their answers in that which transcends the here and now, for all that is within the here and now ultimately prove to be unsatisfactory—insufficient and unable to provide the answers to life's questions.

Questions are followed by answers. The only answers that suffice regarding the core meanings of life are those that require the existence of that which transcends the here and now, and that favors God.

This reality favors God's existence over his non-existence.

An Aside

The neuroscientist Richard Davidson published research indicating that meditative people have better coordinated neural networks than those who do not meditate—thus giving those who meditate a heightened sense of self-awareness—One is less likely to believe in God, a profound interior notion, if one has a poor awareness of the self! [102]

21

FILLING THE EMPTINESS

If God did not exist, it would be necessary to invent him. [103]
—Voltaire

We know from experience that belief in God fills an emptiness.

Atheists are fully aware that belief in God brings about fulfillment: Marx felt belief in God was an opiate to assuage; Feuerbach and Freud saw it as a psychological projection that gave consolation. Some view it as a delusion of happiness. For Persinger, God is a "built-in pacifier."

We have an emptiness that seeks to be filled. Many seek to fill this emptiness and sense of restlessness with wealth, honor, fame, glory, power, bodily health, pleasure, and so forth. Yet human experience shows us that these things do not fill the emptiness. History has shown us that only belief in God can fill the emptiness!

Those who seek wealth, honor, power, etc., to fill the emptiness, and acquire them, find momentary satisfaction, but then the emptiness returns. They thus seek to acquire more wealth, honor, power, etc., so as to recapture some sense of satisfaction, but the emptiness always returns. And the pattern goes on. Why does it go on? What is its end?

Attempts to fill oneself with worldly accomplishments and possessions can only bring about temporary fulfillment. In the end, they leave us empty. And what is the consequence of this emptiness? Studies point to the fact that atheists are among the most unhappy, the most bitter, the most intolerant, the most aggressive, and the most likely to pacify their angst with drugs and alcohol. [104] They are more likely to commit suicide or to die in despair. They echo the angst of Severus, "I have been everything and everything is nothing." [105]

Why does human experience teach us that there is nothing in this world that can give us a remedy for this emptiness? Why does human experience teach us that only a belief in something beyond ourselves and this world can fill this emptiness?

Could this belief in God be a delusion? If it is a delusion, it would have to be a universal delusion held by all but a few. No such delusions exists in our day to day experiences of life. Delusions are usually not universal in nature, but usually affect a few or a group! Minority mindsets or worldviews are more likely to be susceptible to delusions than majority groups. In fact, delusions are usually identified by the majority, not the minority. Given the above, atheism is more likely than theism to be delusional, and to be identified as such. Atheism could be seen as a delusion that attempts to fill an emptiness—an unsuccessful one.

What about those who claim that belief in God is an opiate or built-in-pacifier or psychological projection? These explanations for God-belief are different than the delusion argument. In fact, these explanations help to affirm the belief in God. In other words, how do you explain fulfillment—the filling of the emptiness? Well, it's like an opiate, a drug—but with no withdrawal. It is like a built-in-pacifier—one that never ceases to pacify. It is like a psychological projection that gives continual, never subsiding consolation. Yes this is God, the one who fills the emptiness, the one who medicates us against emptiness, the one who pacifies and consoles us—thus alieving the emptiness. They are, in a sense, synonyms for the religious experience of being fulfilled—without the negative side effects. They are synonyms or alternative descriptions of fulfillment, of filling the emptiness.

Belief in God is not the same as the existence of God, yet experience teaches us that what we innately believe in—as opposed to what we are socialized into believing—finds a correspondence in reality. In fact, many philosophers argue that there has never been an innate belief that has not corresponded to a reality! Belief in God is favored as corresponding to the reality of God.

Filling the emptiness favors the real existence of God over his non-existence. Probability favors God. Human experience favors God's existence over his non-existence.

Emptiness favors atheism. Filling the emptiness favors God!

22

C.S. LEWIS' ARGUMENT FROM DESIRE
(ALSO ARGUED BY ST. AUGUSTINE AND GOETHE)

Creatures are not born with desires unless satisfaction for these desires exist. A baby feels hunger: well, there is such a thing as food. A duckling wants to swim: well, there is such a thing as water. Men feel sexual desire: well, there is such a thing as sex. If I find myself a desire which no experience in this world can satisfy, the most probable explanation is that I was made for another world.[106]
—C.S. Lewis

The more formal explanation of Lewis' argument goes as follows:

1. Every innate desire in us corresponds to a real thing that can satisfy that desire.
2. There exists in us one innate desire which nothing on earth can satisfy.
3. There must, therefore, exist something which is beyond this earth that can satisfy this desire.
4. This something is what we call God.

When discussing desires, Lewis makes a distinction between innate desires and externally conditioned desires.

Innate desires come from our nature; they are inborn and universal—that is, they are common to all healthy people.

Externally conditioned desires are acquired through the external influences of the culture we live in. Unlike innate desires, which are found in all healthy people, externally conditioned desires vary from person to person.

Externally conditioned desires do not necessarily correspond to things that exist. I desire that the United States be protected by the superheroes Batman and Superman. Batman and Superman do not exist.

Innate desires, however, always corresponds to things that exists. As the philosopher Peter Kreeft has explained, echoing the consensus of philosophers, when it comes to innate desires "no one has ever found one case of an innate desire for a nonexistent object."[107] I desire food, food exists. I desire drink, drink exists. I desire knowledge, knowledge exists. Our innate desires therefore correspond to real things.

Human experience teaches us that there exists in us an innate desire which nothing on earth can satisfy. Within every person there is the question: "Is this all there is?" Or in the words of the atheist emperor Severus, "I have had everything, and everything is nothing." There is an emptiness that seeks to be filled, and nothing in this world can fill or satisfy it. Since every innate desire has a corresponding reality, according to the consensus of philosophers, there must be something beyond this world that fulfills this innate desire that nothing in this world can satisfy. The desire for God fulfills that innate desire that nothing in this world can satisfy. As the great Augustine explained, echoing Psalm 62 and the hearts of all those who have sought and have found, "Only in God is my soul at rest."

How do we address those who claim they have no such innate desire within them for something which is beyond this earth that can satisfy what this world cannot satisfy? Those who claim no such innate desire are either repressing such a desire or are dysfunctional in their nature, for the desire of that which is beyond this world has always existed in every human being from the beginning of time--even Neanderthals had such an innate desire according to evolutionists.

One may argue that evolution has inbred this innate desire into human beings, and that this innate desire for God's existence happens to be the only inbred, innate desire that does not correspond to a reality or real thing.

Is this possible, maybe; but this would make the innate desire for God the only innate desire in the world that has no corresponding reality! Thus the likelihood of God's existence based on innate desires favors the existence of God.

23
DESCARTES' INTUITION ARGUMENT

Certainly, the idea of God, or a supremely perfect being, is one that I find within me just as surely as the idea of any shape or number. [108]

Rene Descartes argued that the idea of God could only come about because God caused it to come about.

Descartes' argument can very well be called an argument from intuition. The existence of God, for Descartes, is self-evident for those who meditate on his possibility. It is intuitive because the notion of the existence of God is a "clear and distinct" perception in every human person—for some, such as atheists, yet to be discovered through a meditative, self-reflective disposition.

In our day to day experiences, every clear and distinct innate idea of something that we believe corresponds to a real thing *does in fact exist.*

But what about some ancients who believed in the god Zeus? It may be argued that ancient pagans clearly and distinctly perceived of the idea of a god Zeus corresponding to a real god Zeus. The reality is that the ancients clearly and distinctly believed in an innate idea of a being beyond mere humanness as a being that corresponded to a real being. And rightly so. They did not, however, clearly and distinctly perceive of Zeus as Zeus or as the Romans would name him, Jupiter. The idea of a thunder sounding, lightning throwing, sexually promiscuous, childbearing god is not an innate idea of a being that must correspond to a real being, no more than Santa Claus or a unicorn is. These ideas of beings are neither clear nor distinctly perceived; they are externally, artificially (culturally, sociologically) conditioned. All cultures and societies have believed in something beyond themselves, something supernatural (innate realities), but not all cultures and societies were and are aware of Zeus (because Zeus or Jupiter is an externally, artificially taught being)! Who even knows what Zeus looks like and does today?

If one clearly and distinctly perceives that the innate idea of a perfect being must correspond to a real perfect being, then such a perfect being truly, in all probability, exists. Clear and distinct perceptions of innate ideas corresponding to real beings, favors the existence of God over his non-existence.

Advances in the study of consciousness has added greater weight to this argument. If there are experiences of consciousness that cannot be self-produced, and that cannot be explained by a brain-alone, materialistic approach, then the argument from intuition takes on even greater weight.

> After years of research . . . our understanding of various key brain structures and the way information is channeled along neural pathways led us to hypothesize that the brain possesses a neurological mechanism for self-transcendence. The mind remembers mystical experiences with the same degree of clarity and sense of reality that it bestows upon memories of "real" past events. The same cannot be said of hallucinations or dreams. We believe this sense of

realness strongly suggests that the accounts of the mystics are not indications of minds gone astray, but are the proper, predictable neurological result of a stable, coherent mind willing itself toward a higher spiritual plane. [109]
—Andrew Newberg, Radiologist, Neurologist

24
SPIRITUAL DEVELOPMENT—DEFICIENT OR NOT

The most beautiful emotion we can experience is the mystical. It is the power of all true art and science. He to whom this emotion is a stranger, who can no longer wonder and stand rapt in awe, is as good as dead.[110]
—Einstein, Physicist

After years of research . . . our understanding of various key brain structures and the way information is channeled along neural pathways led us to hypothesize that the brain possesses a neurological mechanism for self-transcendence. The mind remembers mystical experiences with the same degree of clarity and sense of reality that it bestows upon memories of "real" past events. The same cannot be said of hallucinations or dreams. We believe this sense of realness strongly suggests that the accounts of the mystics are not indications of minds gone astray, but are the proper, predictable neurological result of a stable, coherent mind willing itself toward a higher spiritual plane.[111]
—Andrew Newberg, Radiologist, Neurologist

The hope that neuroscience would quickly identify some simple materialistic [atheistic] explanation for the spiritual nature of the human has failed and will continue to fail . . . Materialists [atheists] are compelled to go on looking for God genes, helmets, spots, and modules indefinitely.[112]
—Mario Beauregard, Neuroscientist

Spiritual Triggers

For God-believers, the spiritual is nothing other than living in harmony with perceived truth.[113] In other words, for God believers, innate to the individual is the pull toward spiritual perfection, truth. It is for this reason that religions that acknowledge supernatural realities often share similar spiritual journeys.

There are universal wants that need to be met. All people desire renewal, forgiveness, community, peace, meaning, purpose, immortality, salvation, and a means for authentic living. Everyone needs a means to deal with the trials and tribulations of life. Everyone wants to make their joys more joyful and their times of difficulty easier to overcome. Because the world and people face similar challenges and desires, it is not unusual to see similarities in religious beliefs.

The concept that the divine, the spiritual, God, makes the person fully human is in direct conflict with atheist thought, as the words of Marx exemplify: "Man makes religion, religion does not make man."[114] The eternal truth of spiritual growth is in direct opposition to Marx's paradigm.

Neuroscience's identification of spiritual triggers that are set off by prayer, meditation, and religious worship makes it clear that religious people have a different experience of the world, one that is not static, one that can grow with prayer, meditation and religious worship.[115] This begs the question: Are atheists failing to trigger their spiritual potential? And if one does not trigger one's spiritual potential, how can one possibly grasp even the possibility of God?

Let us now examine the general and universal pattern of spiritual development. Let us begin with what is referred to as an "awakening."

Awakening

People are often awakened to the possibility of God because God gives them a sense of meaning and purpose in life. One recognizes that one must be more than some complex organism that is born, lives, struggles, and dies in emptiness. For such people, there must be more to life than mere existence, than mere survival. Life needs purpose and meaning, a purpose and meaning that transcends the here and now. For such people life without God leads to disintegration.

Once awakened to God one may choose to progress and develop spiritually or one may simply choose to remain at an infantile stage of spiritual development.

This is a dangerous stage. In the spirit of Christianity's Saint Paul, the old self is still dominating the new self. It is in this stage that atrocities can run rampant.

As one progresses in the spiritual life, the desire for truth comes to the fore. Such people seek truth in life, no matter where they may find it. Such people find great comfort in God for he is the goal of their quest, truth itself. Hence, life becomes for such individuals a delving into the mysteries of God, which consumes the entirety of their lives and gives them their ultimate joy.

Atheists limit their quest for truth to science or the relativistic self. They avoid the transcendent, yet that is where the apex of ultimate truth itself is found!

The hunger for the good comes to fruition. The former atheist, Malcolm Muggeridge, a renowned reporter for the BBC, was such a person in many aspects. It was in seeing the good that was in the heart of Mother Teresa of Calcutta that he was able to find Christ. In Mother Teresa he saw Jesus Christ, and his life would never be the same. God is good, and those who have found authentic goodness have found God.

Finally, the hunger and desire for beauty comes to the forefront. The beauty of creation, the handprint of God, is beginning to be perceived. As one progresses, all of creation is marked by the beauty and providence of God. To find authentic beauty is to find the source of all beauty, God. (See Aquinas' argument from gradation).

As one grows one develops a healthy balance between thinking and feeling, between grasping the transcendent and the immanent. Psychologists

Fowler, Piaget and Kohlberg, all familiar to students of elementary and middle school education, empirically point to how the brain expresses stages of faith--one where moral development, increasing abstraction, and sophistication in one's faith grows as one's cognitive abilities mature. [116]

For the spiritual, one sees life's difficulties and sufferings as moments of purification and perfecting. The old self confronts a newer self. One's behaviors, beliefs, attitudes, and desires become reevaluated. Priorities are reordered. Moral integration begins. A movement from infantile faith and trust which are self-centered start to evolve into a faith that is other-centered. Sins or acts of disharmony--by omission or commission--are easily identified and begin to be conquered. A newer, better self evolves.

Pillars of growth begin to take hold. Humility—which for the spiritual is nothing other than self-knowledge in the presence of the transcendent—love, silence, and a desire to be detached of all so as to love all as all is meant to be loved develops. One begins to surrender and trust in that which is beyond the self.

Predominant faults and inclinations become illuminated. Alienation, anger, bitterness, meaningless boredom, depression, an inability to get along with others, and other self-destructive behaviors become illuminated and removed. One's blind sides become illuminated and eliminated.

Dark Night

As one progresses, one encounters a darkness. This is a time to choose: Do I go forward or do I allow myself to fall back? If one decides to move on, a dark night or deep and profound spiritual purification takes place.

This darkness is marked by vulnerability. Prayer and the spiritual life seem dry, without consolation. One often feels rejected by family, friends, and society. Life can even seem to be falling apart. Often the sense of God disappears. For the spiritually astute, this darkness is where God is most active, purifying the imagination, memory, intellect, and will. One is beginning to experience God by means of the spirit as opposed to the senses. The lower forms of prayer such as petition and meditation are being transformed into the higher forms of prayer such as contemplation. One becomes aware of whether one is experiencing this darkness due to psychological problems—despair, illness—or through an authentic cleansing of the soul—marked by an unwavering faith, hope, and love amidst trials and suffering.

This stage of spiritual darkness is a stage that most God-believers do not like to go through, and it is why most God-believers either back away or fail to move beyond it.

Illumination and Enlightenment

For those who persevere into and through this darkness, illumination and enlightenment follows. It is at this stage that the flourishing of the virtues come to fruition. The supernatural virtues of faith, hope, and love, and the cornerstone virtues of prudence, temperance, justice, and fortitude flourish. Pride, lust, unjustified anger, gluttony, envy, sloth, and inordinate cravings are slowly eradicated. It is at this stage, often referred to as the Illuminative stage, that great works of social justice are undertaken.

Prayer at this level moves into the sphere of contemplation, from the prayer of quiet to the prayer of simple union, and finally to the prayer of transforming union (where the mystics enter into a spiritual betrothal and a spiritual marriage with the divine). Peace, quiet, calm, repose, serenity, and rest are the fruits of this experience. Knowledge of realities that transcend the natural means of knowing are infused. One gets a sense that one is in a sphere of existence that is beyond space and time. A deepening, wounding, inflaming, engulfing, inflowing, longing love for the divine and the desire to grow in the image and likeness of that which is loved, the divine, God, matures.

Purification of the Soul and the Mystical

For the few that continue the journey, a final, intense purification is experienced, often referred to as the passive and active purification of the soul.

In this spiritual stage, an excess of God's presence blinds all the faculties of the person so as to purify them. It is in this final purification that one is divested of the defects of the will, reasoning, memory, imagination, and prayer.

One comes through this process a mystic! As Therese of Lisieux described the situation: "In the crucible of trails from within and without, my soul has been refined, and I can raise my head like a flower after a storm and see how the words of the Psalm have been fulfilled: 'The Lord is my Shepherd and there is nothing other that I shall need.'"

The mystical stage is marked by the living out of the heroic virtues and the spiritualization of the senses to heights beyond previous human capacities. It finds a beautiful expression in the prayer of Francis:

> Lord, make me an instrument of your peace. Where there is hatred, let me sow love. Where there is injury, pardon. Where there is doubt, faith. Where there is despair, hope. Where there is darkness, light. Where there is sadness, joy. O Divine Master, grant that I not so much seek to be consoled as to console; to be understood as to understand; to be loved as to love. For it is in giving that we receive; it is in pardoning that we are pardoned; and it is in dying that we are born to eternal life.

The spiritual quest is a quest to be fully human. Atheists, by refusing to participate in or by denying the very nature of the spiritual, are by definition living a less than fully human life. They are failing to trigger their spiritual dimension.

Neuroscience and the Mystical

Neuroscience in recent years has begun studying mystics. A recent study of Carmelite nuns by the famed neuroscientist Mario Beauregard is worth citing. He and his collogues sought to examine whether there was such a thing as a God module, a spot in the brain dedicated to spirituality. The study also sought to examine whether mystical experiences were different from emotional experiences or delusions.

What they discovered was that mystical experiences use many brain regions--the medial orbitofrontal cortex, the right middle temporal cortex, the right inferior and superior parietal lobules, the right caudate, the left medial prefrontal cortex, the left anterior cingulated cortex, the left inferior parietal lobule, the left insula, the left caudate, the left brain stem, and the extrastriate visual cortex. The study clearly put to rest the search for a God-spot or God module.

Brain activity within the minds of the nuns when experiencing mystical states were distinct in nature from those associated with simple emotions and delusions. In the words of Beauregard, "Our objective and subjective data suggest that [religious experiences] are complex multidimensional and mediated by a number of brain regions normally implicated in perception, cognition, emotion, body representation, and self-consciousness."[117]

The fact that many throughout the world move from meaninglessness to purpose, from anger to love, anxiety to peace, self-centeredness to other-centeredness, doubt to faith, despair to hope, darkness to light, disharmony to harmony, disintegration to integration, and sadness to a taste of eternal bliss is a sign of the universality of the experience of and hunger for the divine. It is a journey--viewed by the spiritual--that makes one's joys more joyful and one's times of sufferings easier to overcome.

Fully Human?

What does this generalized universal pattern of spiritual development imply for the atheist? Could it be that the atheist has an underdeveloped brain, or a brain that is underused or under-socialized or even dysfunctional in terms of spirituality? Could it be that this underdeveloped, un-awakened brain is what predisposes atheists--disproportionally according to statistics--toward acts of pride, covetousness, lust, anger, gluttony, envy and sloth? Could this be why the "spiritually advanced" are noted for their humility, generosity, chastity (according to their state in life), mildness, temperance, friendship, and diligence?

If the atheist represses, rejects, or fosters a dormancy in his or her spiritual nature—a universal reality (even Neanderthals were spiritual beings)—then what are the implications that follow?

If wholeness is superior to deficiency, then a God-believer is more fully human than one who lacks or is deficient in an arguably crucial aspect of human life. If the atheist is missing a spiritual nature, or has never developed a spiritual nature, how can he or she believe in God, or access God?

Since an innate belief (as opposed to a socially conditioned belief) in something ordinarily corresponds—or as a consensus of philosophers argue, always corresponds--to a reality, then an innate belief in God more than likely corresponds to the reality of God, especially since wholeness is superior to deficiency, particularly when accessing reality. [118]

Therefore, the existence of God is favored over his non-existence.

An Aside

Twenty years of spiritual direction and counseling have shown me that those who cease praying fall into doubt and worldliness, sometimes even practical atheism. The cure to this fall is prayer. Prayer clearly activates what was previously not activated in the brain. A more active brain is a healthier and more effective brain, with healthier outcomes. The brain can in many ways be seen as spiritual by nature and evolution.

25

NEWMAN'S ARGUMENT FROM CONSCIENCE

Atheists and theists recognize the existence of conscience. Atheists such as Nietzsche view it as primarily a biological and/or cultural product of evolution. Theists, like the legendary Cardinal John Henry Newman, argue that conscience is a convincing argument for the existence of God that cannot simply be explained by biology or culture.

In the words of Newman:

> If, as is the case, we feel responsibility, are ashamed, are frightened, at transgressing the voice of conscience, this implies that there is One to whom we are responsible, before whom we are ashamed, whose claims upon us we fear. If, on doing wrong, we feel the same tearful, brokenhearted sorrow which overwhelms us on hurting a mother; if, on doing right, we enjoy the same sunny serenity of mind, the same soothing, satisfactory delight which follows on our receiving praise from a father, we certainly have within us the image of some person, to whom our love and veneration looks, in whose smile we find happiness, for whom we yearn, toward whom we direct our pleadings, in whose anger we are troubled and waste away. These feelings in us are such as require for their exciting cause an intelligent being: we are not affectionate toward a stone . . . [There are causes of feelings which are not found in earthly intellectual beings]: The wicked flees when no one pursueth: Why does he flee? Whence his terror? Who is it that he sees in solitude, in darkness, in the hidden chambers of the heart? If the eliciting or exciting cause of these emotions does not belong to this visible world, the Object [the intellectual being] to which his perception is directed must be Supernatural and Divine . . . .[119]

Conscience is not awakened, or elicited by any earthly object such as a stone. We do not feel the twinges of conscience after tripping over a rock. Objects can attract and repel us, but they do not do so in the same manner that feelings associated with conscience do. The feelings uniquely associated with conscience are related to our human interactions with intelligent beings. In other words, conscience is elicited or awakened by a live being, not an inanimate object.

Some intelligent beings (i.e., a mother, a father) elicit deep twinges of emotions within us. If the intelligent being from whom conscience is elicited cannot be found on earth, in this visible world, then this intelligent being must be found in that which transcends this visible world: "The wicked flees when no one pursueth; Why does he flee? Whence his terror? Who is it that he sees in solitude, in darkness, in the hidden chambers of the heart?" God?

Conscience is a convincing and converging argument for the existence of God. Conscience favors God.

26
ANSWERED PRAYERS?

Are prayers answered?

Prayer is not the manipulating of God to acquire something that God did not know we needed; quite the contrary, God knows all, including our needs. He knows what we will ask and all the free will decisions we will make in advance. He knows what we need and how it fits within his providence—that sphere of representativeness that is between two extremes, predestination and absolute, undeterred free will.

Why pray if God is all knowing? We pray to show our need, our love, and our dependence upon God, not because God needs this love or dependence, but because we do. We pray because it teaches us about ourselves and our priorities? We pray because it develops our spiritual brain, and thus brings light, happiness, and peace into our life and world.

Atheists often argue against the belief in God because answered prayers are not provable objectively. Prayer, unfortunately for the atheist, is not so simplistic a concept.

For the believer prayers are answered, but not necessarily in the manner in which one expects the prayer to be answered. Prayers are answered in such a fashion that one's eternal destiny is always in the forefront. Prayer is always answered with the understanding that this earthly life is but a blink of the eye when compared to eternity. Prayer is always understood from the perspective of the present and future good of the world and with the understanding that all prayers are interconnected—at the level of the individual, the community, and the world.

When we look upon the history of our prayers and desires, we see that our prayers were in fact answered, but most often in ways we did not expect. This is beautifully illustrated in the words of an unknown civil war soldier:

> I asked for strength that I might achieve; I was made weak that I might learn humbly to obey. I asked for health that I might do greater things; I was given infirmity that I might do better things. I asked for riches that I might be happy; I was given poverty that I might be wise. I asked for power that I might have the praise of men; I was given weakness that I might feel the need of God. I asked for all things that I might enjoy life; I was given life that I might enjoy all things. I got nothing that I asked for, but everything that I had hoped for. Almost despite myself, my unspoken prayers were answered; I am, among all men, most richly blessed. [120]

Are prayers answered? If prayers are answered, then consciousness is infused with transcendentalism and with immaterialism.

Since the beginning of recorded history, people have prayed, and have believed in answered prayers. If prayers were not felt to be answered, at one point in history, prayers would have been abandoned as part of a bankrupt belief system.

The action of prayer, whether God exists or not, at the very least, leads to the development of the brain—an advantage. In recent years, several neuro-scientists have published research indicating that meditative people have better coordinated neural networks than those who do not meditate—thus giving those who meditate a heightened sense of self-awareness—One cannot believe in God, a profound interior notion, if one has a poor awareness of the self! [121]

If prayers are answered, then God exists.

Personal experience favors the existence of answered prayers over non-answered prayers. Personal experience, therefore, favors the existence of God over his non-existence.

27

AQUINAS' ARGUMENT FROM GRADATION

[A way to prove the existence of God] is based on the gradation observed in things. Some things are better, truer, more excellent than others. Such comparative terms describe varying degrees of approximation to a superlative.... Something therefore is the truest and best and most excellent of things, and hence the most fully in being.... Now when many things possess some property in common, the one most fully possessing it causes it in the others.... Something therefore causes in all other things their being, their goodness, and whatever other perfection they have. And this is what we call God. [122]
—Newman

Real degrees of real perfection presuppose the existence of that perfection itself (the Perfect Being). [123]
—Newman

How do we know what is better, truer or more excellent unless we can distinguish between levels or gradations of goodness, truth, excellence, etc.? Anything that has gradations must have a perfection, a superlative, from which all lesser gradations can be observed.

What is this superlative?

What is best described as the fullness of goodness, truth, excellence or any other superlative?

Everything of human origin is flawed. God is by definition perfect, the Superlative!

If there were no superlative, then there would be an infinite regress of gradations. Human experience teaches us that all regressions are finite. Therefore, God must be the source and summit of the gradation, particularly since everything of human origin is flawed.

Thus: God is not simply good; he is goodness itself. He is subsistent goodness. God is not simply true; he is truth itself. He is subsistent truth. God is not simply harmonious; he is harmony itself. God is not simply excellent; he is excellence itself. He is subsistent excellence, etc.

If it is true that real degrees of real perfection presuppose the existence of that perfection itself, the perfect being, then that perfect being—in an imperfect world—is more likely than less likely that which is in this world but transcends this world—and we call this entity God.

Gradations in perfection favor the existence of God over his non-existence.

28
ARGUMENT FROM FREE WILL

Free will presumes the existence of God. Atheism presumes determinism, or a convoluted form of determinism that gives the impression of free will. [124]

For many atheists, such as new atheist Daniel Dennett, we are "big, fancy robots," supercomputers absent of free will. (But Daniel, robots and computers have a creator!)

For such people as Dennett the brain is a fixed system which has either a "god spot," "god center," "god module," "god circuit," "god virus," "soft spot," "mystical gene," "god gene," etc. Some atheists assume that there is an organ (s), gene (s), or a programmed basis for spirituality and God. Just as the world can be understood in a purely naturalistic understanding of reality, so too, they argue, can the brain and consciousness.

Oxygen and hydrogen, they continue their argument, do not combine by free will or choice in producing water. They follow the natural laws. Every component to our being, likewise, in a naturalistic system, is bound to natural laws which excludes the possibility of free will or choice.

Free will cannot exist in such a robotic, deterministic, fixed, naturalistic brain and consciousness.

If it can be proved—or at least argued as more probable—that free will exists, then the probability for God's existence is favored over his non-existence—for in a purely naturalistic vision of life, free will is not possible.

When we examine our daily human experiences we notice the following:

a. When we speak it appears self-evident that our speech is free.
b. We do not always act in the same way in the same circumstances—or at least what we perceive to be the same circumstances.
c. The people we observe do not behave the same way in the same circumstances—or at least what we perceive to be the same circumstances.
d. We act toward the same prohibitions or exhortations differently in the same circumstances—or at least what we perceive to be the same circumstances.
e. Relating to one another also shows we do so differently under the same circumstances—or at least what we perceive to be the same circumstances.
f. The extreme variety of lifestyle choices favors free will.
g. The rush to judgment, rather than the pondering over the facts, which we all fall prey to, favors free will.
h. Monitoring and evaluating our thoughts prior to acting favors the existence of free will.

i. If there is no free will then there is no right or wrong. Yet cultures and races throughout the world hold to universal rights and wrongs. Why? Are these simply universally inbred physical, causal, psychological and biological predeterminers?

j. There would be a superficial, if any, meaning or purpose to life if there were no free will. This is counterintuitive.

k. Human virtue is available to all. Human virtues are firm and stable attitudes, dispositions, and habits of the intellect and will acquired through human effort. The primary function of virtue is to bring human actions and passions under the dominion of reason. Heroic virtue is that which transcends the natural virtues and elevates them to higher levels. The acquisition of virtue is more likely due to free will than determinism.

l. Advances in the study of the brain has overturned the old simplistic, static-fixed-system brain approach. Neuroscientists are now aware of what is often called the neuroplasticity of or plasticity or malleability of the brain. The brain is subject to changes in neural pathways and synapses as the person responds to changes in behavior, environment, thinking, emotions, and bodily injury. The brain, in all its complexity, allows for a multiplicity of reactions to external and internal stimuli. The processing, reacting, and choosing among the multiplicity of internal and external stimuli points to the possibility of free will more than a deterministic vision of the person, and of the world. Nature, nurturing, perceivably random events, present and past experiences, and projected desires not only modify the brain but can be modified by the brain's inherent ability to project consequences and prospective choices. The advent of modern neuroscience, besides proving the neuroplasticity of the brain, has also shown a growing likelihood, for many neuroscientists, for a biological basis for free will. That is, animals, and thus humans, seem to have a built-in biological trait that enables free will. The neuroscientist Bjorn Brembs summarizes the research of many in the field:

[There is] accumulating evidence . . . towards a general organization of brain function that incorporates flexible decision-making on the basis of complex computations negotiating internal and external processing. The adaptive value of such an organization consists of being unpredictable for competitors, prey or predators, as well as being able to explore the hidden resource deterministic automats would never find. At the same time, this organization allows all animals to respond efficiently with tried-and-tested behaviors to predictable and reliable stimuli . . . . The comparatively recent evidence indicates that one common ability of most if not all brains is to choose among different behavioral options even in the absence of differences in the environment and perform genuinely novel [free] acts. [125]

With the advances in modern neuroscience, scientists are moving toward alleged biological causes for free will (i.e., a biological free will trait). In other words, atheists intuitively seem to recognize the reality of free will, and are thus seeking to explain it in purely materialistic manners.

Unfortunately, the atheist attempts at proving free will from a purely atheistic and materialistic approach is inadequate and even faulty. In reality, these attempts at affirming a biological trait for free will are simply an affirmation of the obviousness of free will in human actions. Yet these studies in no way conclusively prove free will. In fact, Brembs' argument, and those of his colleagues, are simply an intricate, convoluted, and elaborate form of determinism. True free will requires that which transcends the naturalistic, materialistic dimensions of the human person and his consciousness, God. Materialistic atheists are in a dilemma.

Those who affirm free will and those who deny it, recognize that the "consciousness problem" cannot be divorced from their work. That is, what is consciousness and how does it work or interact with the brain?

All of these arguments from human experience—what we know first and best, as Aristotle would say—and advances in neurology seem to favor the reality of free will.

Our shared human experience of life, the new understanding of the brain, and the now understood neuroplasticity, plasticity, or malleability of the brain, while favoring free will's operation, is not an absolute assurance of free will. But when human experience and the neuroplasticity of the brain is combined with the nature of consciousness, and its likely transcendental dimension (see the above argument on consciousness) then free will is most likely. The interaction of brain matter, consciousness and its transcendence, and the likelihood of intuitively free will choices make the existence of God more likely than less likely.

Free will favors the existence of God—for free will, by its very nature, implies an ability to break from a deterministic, naturalistic, atheistic vision of the will. Free will implies the ability to transcend determinism—in its simplistic form and in its complex, convoluted form. God, by nature, could not be bound to determinism, to a boxed-in mind.

The likelihood of free will favors the existence of God over his non-existence.

And if there is no free will, or if there is a built-in biological trait for free will, this does not affirm atheism, it simply affirms in a more clear fashion God as the intelligent designer. In fact, a closed-system-organism, devoid of the transcendental, yet one that gives the impression to the majority of people the power of free will decision-making, and perceived transcendental realities, would have to be so intricate, convoluted, and elaborate that design by a designer would have to be favored. A God-guided, designed evolutionary process would be the only possible explanation for so complex a phenomenon (3.7 billion years cannot explain the existence of the cell; how would it be able to explain such a complex system?).

God can exist with or without free will. Atheism cannot! Atheism can only be a truism in a deterministic understanding of the world.

Do you have free will or are you an intricate automaton?

29
LEIBNIZ'S NECESSARY EXPLANATION
AND PERFECTION ARGUMENT

Necessary Explanation—First Argument (An Argument from Contingency)

Why is there something rather than nothing? In our day to day experiences something cannot come from nothing: something comes from something. If there were nothing there could not be something. Therefore there must be something for something. The universe is something.

Every existing thing has an explanation for its existence. And since every existing thing has an explanation rather than no explanation for its existence, then what is the explanation for the existence of the universe?

Now it may be argued that the universe always existed, with no beginning. Human experience, however, teaches us that things that exist have a source for their existence. If this is so, then the question must be posed: "What exists without an explanation for its existence?" *Existence itself, subsistent existence.* And we call this God.

The existence of the universe favors the existence of God as its explanation, for *existence itself* is the only "thing" that cannot be put into existence. *Existence itself* is the only "thing" that can stop an infinite regress. *Existence itself* is what we call God.

Necessary Perfection—Second Argument

God is by definition a being having all perfections. It is a simple and absolute property—that which expresses without any limits whatever it does express. *Existence itself, subsistent existence,* is a perfection, for nothing can be added to it or subtracted from it; nothing can make it better or worse. *Existence* is the fullness of what it is-- existence. Things exists or do not. There is nothing that is a little bit in existence and a little bit out of existence. Therefore existence is part of the essence of all things.

Since existence is part of the essence of all things, or a thing, it is a necessary reality for any "thing" to exist. And since this necessary reality, *existence itself,* or *subsistent existence*, is without addition or subtraction, it is a perfect reality. Since such a reality exists, or else there would be no existing realities, and this reality is a perfection, then this reality is by definition God. This necessary being for anything to exist, existence, is a perfection. This is by definition God.

The probability of God's existence is favored over his non-existence. [126]

30
ANSELM'S ARGUMENT (REVISED)

The concept of God is innately understood as "something-than-which-nothing-greater-can-be-thought." Even the atheist understands the concept for it is innately understood by all human beings as the concept for God.

The question: Does the concept that "something-than-which-nothing-greater-can-be-thought" only exist in the mind and not in reality? Innate concepts—as opposed to culturally, socially conditioned concepts—always correspond to reality. Given this truism, why would "something-than-which-nothing-greater-can-be-thought" be the only innately held belief that does not correspond to reality?

"Something-than-which-nothing-greater-can-be-thought," our concept of God, favors God's existence over his non-existence. [127]

31
NECESSARY GAP FILLER FOR A FINITE MIND

Given the limits to the human brain and its evolutionary future, God may very well be the only one who will be able to fill the gaps that human knowledge will never be able to grasp!

God has been used to fill in the gaps of knowledge (i.e., for Newton, God was the one who corrected the abnormalities in the orbits of the planets). Obviously gap filling in such a way is poor logic and poor science.

But before we become worshippers of science—as some atheists consciously or subconsciously are—science has always had its own gap fillers. In fact, there are more historical gap fillers attributed to science than to any other endeavor of study.

In the past, scientists argued that the liver and not the heart circulated blood and that blood was consumed like a fuel in an engine by the organs. The astronomer Ptolemy argued that the earth was the center of the universe. Galileo argued for round orbits around the sun, but in fact the orbits are elliptical. Scientists felt that infections were caused by "bad air." Others believed that diseases were caused by an imbalance of blood, phlegm, and bile. Some scientists postulated a phenomenon called "phlogiston" as responsible for the air we breathe and for the sustaining of fires—as opposed to oxygen. Scientists argued that proteins were the mechanism of heredity as opposed to DNA. Some argued that there was a somewhere yet to be found elixir that would prolong and renew life. Some argued that sperm came from the brain. Some scientists argued that elements could morph into others as lead could morph into gold through the use of a "philosopher stone." Science today has resorted to aliens, multi-worlds, memes, life-seeded asteroids or meteors, panspermia, etc., to describe the origins of life and consciousness. These are as hypothetical as angels moving stars.

Science has more gap fillers than theists!

Some worshippers of science, however, argue that once science finds it has made a mistake, it changes its view or views. Well the same thing applies to believers in God—if God is truth itself, then reason and faith cannot contradict each other. Either the faith is wrong or the science is—both must be in conformity; otherwise truth becomes relative and therefore non-existent.

Now we are left with the questions: Is the human mind so powerful, or will it be so powerful by evolution, that it will be able to comprehend all things? Is the human mind, in other words, the greatest possible mind? Is it capable or will it ever be capable of being all-knowing? If the answer is no, then the mind will always be limited; then the mind will always need gap fillers to explain what ultimately it will never be able to explain.

In the end, at the apex of human knowledge and the power of the human mind, there will still be mysteries beyond human comprehension. Just like a cockroach will never be able to know what we know, we will not be able to know that which is beyond the capacity of our brain's present or future power.

Thus "mystery" will only be able to be filled with God or with some hypothesized, but inevitably, eternally unverifiable theory.

We are left with some profound questions, including, "What will always exist beyond the mind's comprehension?" What should we call this reality beyond our finite-mind?

We can call it anything we want, but in the end, the ultimate-final phenomenon beyond our mind's comprehension will be a superior actuality: This ultimate first-cause transcendent actuality would be by definition God!

Given the mind's nature, probability favors God's existence over his non-existence. For whatever transcends the mind's limits is and would be by definition more likely than less likely God.

32
AUGUSTINIAN INFLUENCED ARGUMENT
FROM THE PERSON TO GOD

If there is anything superior to the human person (understood universally), then that reality would be a superior being. If there is nothing superior to the human person, then there is no superior being to the human person.

If there is a superior being to the human person it would either be God or another superior being other than God. If there is nothing superior to the superior being, then the superior being is by definition what we call God. If there is something greater than the superior being, then that superior being to the superior being to the human person would be the ultimate superior being. If we continue the pattern we must end up with the ultimate superior being where no other beings could be superior. This is God.

An Aside

Innate, inborn, and universal to human consciousness is the belief in such a superior being. This belief is only lost when external conditions make a person think otherwise.

Innate beliefs—non-conditioned beliefs—correspond to realities.

Since innate beliefs relate to real things, then the innate belief in God favors his existence over his non-existence. [128]

33
BRAIN IN VAT ARGUMENT

Is it possible, reader, that you are simply a brain in a vat of bio-chemical fluid? Attached to your brain in the vat are wires devoted to a highly advanced computer. This morning you woke up, drove to work, worked and socialized, drove home, met the wife and children at the door, then sat down to read this book.

The problem is that you are simply a brain in a vat—there was no waking up, no driving to work, no working and socializing, no driving home, no wife or family, no sitting down and reading. These experiences, what you supposedly saw, heard, smelled, tasted, and touched during your day were all experiences programed directly into your brain in a vat of fluid by mad scientists. You are simply a brain in a vat.

We are not brains in vats, not because we have absolutely perfect arguments that we are not, but because it is self-evident, intuitive, instinctive, innate, palpable, imaginable, supposable, and presumable.

The idea of a God or his existence has always been, and continues to be in healthy individuals, not because it is provable with absolute conviction (at least to most minds) but because it is self-evident, intuitive, instinctive, innate, palpable, imaginable, supposable, and presumable.

In a world where, hypothetically, no absolute certainty can be assured— we may be brains in vats—the possible existence of God is more likely than his non-existence because of his self-evident and innately known presence.

I can choose to stand in the middle of the highway and wait for an eighteen wheel truck to come roaring down the road towards me. I can't prove with absolutely certain arguments that such a truck exists, nor that it is roaring down the road towards me. But you can be assured, that I am going to get out of the way! Its roaring down the road is self-evident! That's certain!

CONCLUSION: PASCAL'S WAGER

To believe in God places one in a winning situation.

- To believe in God makes one happy in this life (whether this happiness is real, a delusion, a Marxian opiate, or a Freudian-Feuerbachian projection) and upon death one is either right or wrong. If wrong, there will be no awareness of being wrong. If right there will be eternal life and bliss.

To not believe in God places one in a losing situation.

- To not believe in God brings about a life chasing after unattainable happiness in this life, and upon death, if one is right one will never know. If one is wrong, then eternal life is lost, and one's earthly journey was wasted: Severus whispered, "I have been everything and everything is nothing!" Thomas Paine explained, "I would give worlds if I had them . . . . I am at the edge of hell all alone." Carlile sniveled, "I am as good as without hope, a sad old man gazing into the final chasm." Sir Thomas Scott sobbed "Until this moment, I thought there was neither God nor hell . . . " Edward Gibbon despaired, "All is dark and doubtful." Sir Francis Newport cried, "All is over, all is lost." Hobbes said, "I am about to take a fearful leap into the dark . . . ." Marx shouted to his nurse, "Get out, get out. Let me die alone." Taleran admitted, "I am suffering the pangs of the damned." Vollney cried incessantly "My God, My God, My God . . . "Meravue exclaimed, "Give me opium that I may not think of eternity." Aldamont summarized the atheist lifestyle best, "Life was hell, and there is another hell ahead."[129]

Bet, wager on God. It is the best bet![130]

EPILOGUE: PROBLEM OF SUFFERING

Atheists detest suffering and often deny God's existence because of suffering. Thus, atheists, I argue, are in need of a new paradigm, a shift in perspective.

Suffering is not a curse or tragedy—whether at the individual or societal level: suffering is a gift, a grace, a blessing. Without suffering we cannot be authentically human.

Without suffering we become slaves to self-will and self-infatuation. We develop an obsession with controlling the "here and now," which always fails. Without suffering we would be destined to a life of slavery.

Suffering is the key that unshackles that which enslaves. Suffering is the means to freedom. Suffering reminds us of our powerlessness, finitude, and our limitations. It reminds us our fragility and the brevity of life, and ultimately our eternal destiny.

Suffering forces us to confront reality. It strips us to the core of who we are and then asks, "Are we happy with who we have found?"

Thus suffering entails conversion and a revelation. We are not the same after we have suffered. Who we continue to become depends on how much we allow suffering to purge us of our superficialities and our divided nature.

It is only when we are purged of the superficial, the delusional, the repressed that we can become authentically human. It is in the purging process that we find our meaning and purpose in life, that we find the answers to the essential questions in life.

Suffering is transformative; it is freeing and enlightening. It is a must, a grace, a necessity for humanness. Suffering addresses the essential questions in life and offers us a pathway to light, happiness and peace.

To not have suffered is to not have lived!

And if life is eternal, as I believe, then suffering is simply that aspect in life that prepares us for eternity, not as a surprise but as a gift.

The great theologian Karl Rahner marked the difference between a believer's vision of suffering and a non-believers: "[A believer] is a person who accepts without reservations the whole of concrete human life with all its adventures, its absurdities, and its incomprehensibilities. A real non-[believer], on the other hand, a person who could not even be called an "implicit [believer]" in the ultimate depths of the way he lives out human existence, is characterized precisely by the fact that he does not muster this unconditional acceptance of human existence . . . . [The atheist] is characterized by the fact that he does not muster this unconditional acceptance of human existence."[131]

The non-believer is called to a paradigm shift.

Notes

INTRODUCTION

1. Thomas Aquinas quotes come from *Summa Theologiae: A Concise Translation*, ed. and trans. Timothy McDermott (Westminster: Christian Classics, 1989); (Pt. I, Q. 2, Art. 3). See also Brian Davies, *Thomas Aquinas' Summa Theologiae: A Guide and Commentary, 1st Edition*, (Oxford University Press, 2014); Edward Feser, *Aquinas: A Beginner's Guide* (Oxford: OneWorld, 2009); James Ross, *Thomas Aquinas, Summa Theologiae*, "Christian Wisdom Explained Philosophically" in *The Classics of Western Philosophy: A Reader's Guide*, ed. J.E. Garcia (Oxford: Blackwell Publishing), 165; Etienne Gilson, *The Christian Philosophy of Saint Thomas Aquinas* (Indiana: University of Notre Dame Press, 1994); Bernard McGinn, *Thomas Aquinas' Summa Theologiae* (Princeton: Princeton University Press, 2014); Ralph McInerny, *A First Glance at St. Thomas Aquinas* (Indiana: University of Notre Dame Press, 1996); Jean Pierre Torrell, *Saint Thomas*, vol.1, trans. Robert Royal (Catholic University, 1996); "Thomas Aquinas," *The New Schaff-Herzog Encyclopedia*, vol. XI, 422–7.

2. Peter Kreeft, *The Summa of the Summa* (San Francisco: Ignatius Press, 1990), 63; (Pt. I, Q. 2, Art. 3).

3. The empiricists such as Locke, Berkeley and Hume reject the belief in the "innate." Their beliefs, however, are so counterintuitive that they can no longer be seen, particularly with the advances of the sciences of psychology, psycho-biology and neurobiology, as credible.

4. Aquinas, *Summa Theologiae*; (Pt. I, Q. 2, Art. 3).

5. Kreeft, 63. Peter Kreeft uses the principle of sufficient reason to support Aquinas' argument: everything that exists has an adequate or sufficient reason to explain it. The universe, for Kreeft, therefore needs an explanation for its existence.

6. Freeman Dyson, *Disturbing the Universe* (New York: Harper and Row, 1979), 250.

7. Quoted in Robert Jastrow, *God and the Astronomers* (New York: W.W. Norton, 2nd edition, 1992), 104. The Big Bang is also referred to academically as the Standard Model or the Friedmann-Lemaitre Model.

8. Adapted from John Pasquini, *The Existence of God* (University Press of America, 2010).

9. For a detailed analysis of multiverse, multi-universe theories, as well as the general physics regarding the various big bang theories I direct you to Robert Spitzer, *New Proofs for the Existence of God: Contributions of Contemporary Physics and Philosophy*, 13–102. The current opinion of scholars favors a single point of origin for the big bang. I have avoided this point because it really does not matter to my argument, even though I acknowledge its implications are spectacular.

10. See John Pasquini, *The Existence of God* (University Press of America, 2010); *Atheist Persona: Causes and Consequences* (New York: University Press of America, 2014). Also, Martin Bojowald, "What Happened Before the Big Bang?" *Nature Physics* (July 1, 2007): 523–5; Ibid., "Following the Bouncing Universe," *Scientific American*, October 2008; Arvind Borde, "Eternal Inflation and the Initial Singularity," *Physical Review Letters*, vol. 72, no. 21, 2205–8.

11. See William Lane Craig, *The Kalem Cosmological Argument* (New York: Barnes and Nobles, 1979); Ibid., in *The Blackwell Companion to Natural Theology* (Massachusetts: Wiley-Blackwell, 2009); also, Milac Capek, *Concepts of Space and Time: Their Structure and Their Development* (Boston: Reidel, 1976).

12. David Conway, *The Rediscovery of Wisdom* (London: Macmillan, 2000), 125, quoted in Antony Flew, *There is A God: How the World's Most Notorious Atheist Changed His Mind* (New York: HarperOne, 2007), 88. See also the following works in neuroscience: Donald Mackay, *Brains, Machines and Persons* (Grand Rapids: Eerdmans, 1980); Karl Popper and John Eccles, *The Self and Its Brain* (London: Routledge, 1990); Rose Steven, *Against Biological Determinism* (London: Alison and Busby, 1982); ibid., *Not in Our Genes* (Harmondsworth, Penguin, 1992); Roger Sperry, *Science and Moral Priority* (Oxford: Basil Blackwell, 1983). See John Pasquini, *The Existence of God* (University Press of America, 2010); *Atheist Persona: Causes and Consequences* (New York: University Press of America, 2014).

13. Peter B. Medawar, *The Limits of Science* (Oxford: Oxford University Press, 1985), 66.

14. A nice concise summary, which I have adapted, can be found in Casey Luskin, "Top Five Problems with Current Origins of Life Theories," *Life Sciences and Origin of Life News*, December 12, 2012, www.evolution.new.org. See also John Cohen, *Science*, 270 (December 22, 1995), 1925f; National Research Council Space Studies Board, *The Search for Life's Origins* (National Academy Press, 1990). All the current hypothesis for the origin of life, including *abiogenesis* or *biopoiesis*, have proven to be unprovable and unlikely due to the nature of the primordial earth's environment: Life has still not been able to be created from the non-living.

15. David Deamer, "The First Living Systems: A Bioenergetic Perspective," *Microbiology and Molecular Biology Reviews*, 61:239 (1997).

16. Deborah Kelley, "Is it time to throw out the 'Primordial Soup' theory?" NPR (February 7, 2010); National Research Council, *The Limits of Organic Life in Planetary Systems* (Washington: National Academy Press, 2007).

17. Francis Crick, *Life Itself* (New York: Simon and Schuster, 1981), 88.

18. Klaus Dose, "The Origin of Life: More Questions and Answers," *Interdisciplinary Science Reviews* (1988): 13, 348.

19. Greg Easterbrook, "Where did life come from?" *Wired* (February 2007), 108.

20. Antony Flew, *There is a God* (New York: HarperCollins, 2007) 124. Also "My Pilgrimage from Atheism to Theism," *Philosophia Chriti* Vol. 6. No. 2. 2004, 201.

21. Because of the troubling statistical evidence—for atheists--concerning the origin of life, many atheists have resorted to proposing hypothetical multiuniverse theories to explain the origin of life. All attempts (the black hole theory, the string theory approach, the inflationary vacuum or chaotic theory, etc.) have all been discredited. The multiuniverse worldview is nothing more than a "gap-filler," nothing more than pure speculation. The resorting to the multiuniverse theories by atheists is a way of trying to explain away the statistical evidence associated with the intelligent design arguments.

22. Thomas Aquinas quotes come from *Summa Theologiae: A Concise Translation*, ed. and trans. Timothy McDermott (Westminster: Christian Classics, 1989); (Pt. I, Q. 2, Art. 3). See also Brian Davies, Thomas Aquinas's *Summa Theologiae: A Guide and Commentary, 1st Edition*, (Oxford University Press, 2014).

23. Quoted in Dean Radin, *The Conscious Universe* (San Francisco: HarperSanFrancisco, 1997), 265. See John Pasquini, *The Existence of God* (University Press of America, 2010). See also Adraian Boekraad and Henry Tristram, *The Argument from Conscience to the Existence of God* (London: Mill Hill, 1961).

24. John Eccles, *Wonder of Being Human* (New York: Shambhala, 1985), 37.

25. Mario Beauregard, *The Spiritual Brain* (New York: HarperOne, 2007) 109.

26. Wallace B. Allan, *Taboo of Subjectivity* (New York: Oxford University Press, 2004), 3.

27. The following are examples of speculative theories that have attempted to explain the unexplainable. David Chalmers, *The Conscious Mind* (Oxford University Press, 1996); John Eccles, *The Evolution of the Brain* (New York: Routledge, 1989); Nick Herbert, *The Elemental Mind* (Dutton, 1993); Michael Lockwood, *Mind, Brain and the Quantum* (Basil Blackwell, 1989); Alfred Whitehead, *Modes of Thought* (Macmillan, 1939); Fred Wolf, *Mind into Matter* (Moment Point, 2001).

28. Roy Varghese, in Antony Flew, *There is a God* (New York: HarperOne, 2007) appendix 1, 163.

29. Marco Biagini, "Mind and Brain," *Center of Scientific Divulgation about Consciousness*, cf. xoomer.virgilio.it/fedeescienza/mindandbrain, 19-20.

30. See John Pasquini, *The Existence of God* (University Press of America, 2010); *Atheist Persona: Causes and Consequences* (New York: University Press of America, 2014).

31. Thomas Aquinas quotes come from *Summa Theologiae: A Concise Translation*, ed. and trans. Timothy McDermott (Westminster: Christian Classics, 1989), 12–14; (Pt. I, Q. 2, Art. 3). See also Brian Davies, *Thomas Aquinas's Summa Theologiae: A Guide and Commentary, 1st Edition*, (Oxford University Press, 2014).

32. Max Jammer, *Einstein and Religion* (Princeton, NJ: Princeton University Press, 1999), 93.

33. Dembski and McDowell, *Understanding Intelligent Design* (Eugene: Harvest House, 2008); See also Kreeft and Tacelli, *Handbook of Christian Apologetics* (Downer's Grove: Intervarsity Press, 1994; Collins, "A Scientific Argument for the Existence of God," in *Reason for the Hope Within* (Grand Rapids: Eerdmans, 1999).

34. For a study of the cell and its relation to intelligent design I recommend the following: Fazale Rana, *The Cell's Design* (Grand Rapids: Baker Books, 2008). Also, see John Pasquini, *The Existence of God* (University Press of America, 2010).

35. Harold Franklin, *The Way of the Cell* (New York: Oxford University Press, 2001), 205.

36. Quoted in Philip Graham Ryken, *Jeremiah and Lamentations: From Sorrow to Hope* (Wheaton: Crossway, 2001), 100.

37. Antony Flew, *There is a God* (New York: HarperCollins, 2007), 121.

38. Greg Easterbrook, "The New Convergence," *Wired* (December, 2002).

39. For a detailed analysis of multiverse, multi-universe theories, as well as the general physics regarding the various big bang theories, I direct you to Robert Spitzer, *New Proofs for the Existence of God: Contributions of Contemporary Physics and Philosophy* (Cambridge: William B. Eerdmans, 2010), 13–102.

40. See John Pasquini, *The Existence of God* (University Press of America, 2010); *Atheist Persona: Causes and Consequences* (New York: University Press of America, 2014).

41. Adapted from Pasquini, *Atheist Persona* (University Press of America), 104–6, and *The Existence of God* (University Press of America), 30-3. See also R. Collins, "Evidence for Fine-Tuning," in N. Manson, editor, *God and Design: The Teleological Argument and Modern Science* (New York: Routledge), 178-99; Ibid., "Fine-Tuning Argument for Theism," *The Blackwell Companion to Natural Theology* (Oxford: Blackwell, 2009).

42. Cf. Hugh Ross, *The Creator and the Cosmos* (Colorado Springs: NavPress, 2001).

43. Albert Einstein, *Ideas and Opinions*, trans. Sonja Bargmann (New York: Dell, 1973), 49; Jammer, *Einstein and Religion*, 93; *The Quotable Einstein*, ed., Alice Calaprice (Princeton: Princeton University Press, 2005), 196.

44. See John Pasquini, *The Existence of God* (University Press of America, 2010); *Atheist Persona: Causes and Consequences* (New York: University Press of America, 2014).

45. Charles Darwin, *On the Origin of Species* (Cambridge: Harvard University Press, 1964), 189.

46. Stephen Gould, "Punctuated Equilibria: An Alternative to Phyletic Gradualism" in *Models of Paleobiology*, ed. T.J.M. Schopf (San Francisco: Freeman, Cooper and Co., 1972); 82–115.

47. Michael Denton, *Evolution* (Chevy Chase: Adler and Adler, 1986), 289–90.

48. Denton, 61.

49. Stephen Gould, "Punctuated Equilibria" in *Models of Paleobiology*, 82–115.

50. Denton, 157–95; 174

51. *Catholic Encyclopedia*, ed. Stravinkas, 825.

52. C.C. Martindale, *The Message of Fatima* (New York: London, Burns and Oates, 1950), 77-8.

53. Ibid.

54. Ibid. See John Pasquini, *The Existence of God* (University Press of America, 2010); *Atheist Persona: Causes and Consequences* (New York: University Press of America, 2014).

55. I am deeply indebted to the work of Jacalyn Duffin for her rigorous study of more than 1,400 miracles attributed to the intercession of the saints from the 16th century to the present: Jacalyn Duffin, *Medical Miracles: Doctors, Saints, and Healing in the Modern World* (New York: Oxford University Press, 2009).

56. Jacalyn Duffin. 110.

57. Ibid., 76.

58. The following are from the case files of the Medical Bureau of Lourdes. Also found in Pasquini, *The Existence of God* (Lanham: University Press of America, 2010), 46–48.

59. "Religious Involvement, Spirituality and Medicine: Implications for Clinical Practice" Mayo Clinic, 76, 12, 1225. See also John Hick, *The New Frontier of Religion and Science: Religious Experience, Neuroscience, and the Transcendent* (Bassingstoke: Palgrave Macmillan, 2006).

60. B. Spilka, *The Psychology of Religion: An Empirical Approach* (New York: Guilford, 2003).

61. The psycho-social benefits of religious practice by Ona Institute; Larson McCullogh, "Religious Involvement and Mortality," *Health Psychology* 19, 3, 211–22.

62. "Atheism: Contemporary Rates and Patterns," in *Cambridge Companion to Atheism*, ed. Michael Martin (UK: Cambridge University Press, 2005).

63. Mark Holder, University of British Columbia Study, *Springer's Journal of Happiness Studies*: www.sciencedaily.com /releases/2009/01/090108082904.

64. *American Journal of Psychiatry* 161, 2004: 2303-2308; *World Health Organization*, December 2005; "The Mental Health of Students in Higher Education," *Royal College of Psychiatrists*, 2003; Aris Study, 2001. Much of the statistics in the following section are also found in Vox Day's *The Irrational Atheist* (Dallas: Benbella Books, Inc., 2008).

65. Richard Helmstader, *Freedom and Religion in the 19th Century* (Stanford University Press, 1997), 19.

66. Zbigniew Brzezinski , *Out of Control*, (New York: Touchstone, 1995), 17.

67. http://www.icr.org/article/stalins-brutal-faith

68. Vox Day's mastery of statistics is well worth reading in his work *The Irrational Atheist*.

69. John Pasquini, *Atheist Persona* (New York: University Press of America, 2014), 49.

70. Mario Beauregard, *The Spiritual Brain* (New York: HarperOne, 2007), 47.

71. *Religious Belief Systems of Persons with High Functioning Autism*, Boston College, 2015.

72. Andrew Newberg in *Scientific American*, January 16, 2012.

73. Michael Inzlicht, *Psychological Science*, University of Toronto, March 4, 2009.

74. Biographical information from chapters 15 and 16 are adapted by Paul C. Vitz, *The Faith of the Fatherless* (San Francisco: Ignatius Books, 2013).

75. www.cbsnews.com/8301504763.

76. cf. *America Life League*: http://blackquillandink.com/wp-content/uploads/2012/01/margaret-sanger-quotes.pdf. Sanger, *The Woman Rebel*, vol. 1, n. 1, reprinted in *Woman in the New Race* (New York: Brentanos Publishers, 1922).

77. *Atheist Leaders and Immoral Relationships* in conservapedia.com/Atheism, 11: John Bowlby, *The Making and Breaking of Affectional Bonds*, 1979.

78. Ben Macintyre, *Forgotten Fatherland* (Uk: Pan Books, 1993).

79. Brandon Dennis, "Beauty, Truth and Morality," *The Daily of the University of Washington*, February 22, 2007.

80. Atheism, *Conservapedia*, 10: conservapedia.com/Atheism.

81. Quoted in Paul C. Vitz, *The Faith of the Fatherless: The Psychology of Atheism* (Dallas: Spence Publishing, Co., 1999), 137.

82. Biographical information from chapters 15 and 16 are adapted by Paul C. Vitz, *The Faith of the Fatherless* (San Francisco: Ignatius Books, 2013).

83. Ronald Hayman, *Nietzsche: A Critical Life* (New York: Oxford University Press, 1980), 18.

84. Kevin Vost, *From Atheism to Catholicism* (Huntington: Our Sunday Visitor, 210), 30.

85. Walter Kaufmann, *Basic Writings of Nietzsche* (New York: Modern Library, 1992), 169.

86. Cf. "Psychology of Atheism, cf. www.simpletoremember.com/articles/a/pscyology-of-atheism.

87. W.J. Murray, *My Life Without God* (Nashville: Thomas Nelson, 1982), 7.

88. Cf. I am eternally grateful and indebted to the pioneering work on the psychology of atheism by Paul Vitz. Paul Vitz, *The Faith of the Fatherless* (San Francisco: Ignatius Press, 2013), 121-2.

89. Cf. Vitz, 119.

90. "Psychology of Atheism," cf. www.simpletoremember.com/articles/a/pscyology-of-atheism.

91. See John Pasquini, *The Existence of God* (University Press of America, 2010): *Atheist Persona: Causes and Consequences* (New York: University Press of America, 2014).

92. Antoine Lutz, "Long-term Meditators Self-Induce High-Amplitude Gamma Sychrony During Mental Practice," *Proceedings of the National Academy of Sciences USA 101*, no. 46 (November 16, 2004): 16369-73.

93. *Complete Psychological Works of Sigmund Freud* (New York: Norton and Company, 2010); W.W. Meissner, S.J., *Life and Faith* (Washington: Georgetown University Press, 1987). See also Pasquini, *Atheist Persona* (New York: UPA, 2014); Paul Vitz, *Faith of the Fatherless* (San Francisco, Ignatius Press, 2015).

94. *Complete Psychological Works of Sigmund Freud* (New York: Norton and Company, 2010); W.W. Meissner, S.J., *Life and Faith* (Washington: Georgetown University Press, 1987). See also Pasquini, *Atheist Persona* (New York: UPA, 2014); Paul Vitz, *Faith of the Fatherless* (San Francisco, Ignatius Press, 2015).

95. *Complete Psychological Works of Sigmund Freud* (New York: Norton and Company, 2010); Erik Erikson, *The Life Cycle Completed* (New York: Norton and Company, 1998); W.W. Meissner, S.J., *Life and Faith* (Washington: Georgetown University Press, 1987). See also Pasquini, *Atheist Persona* (New York: UPA, 2014); Paul Vitz, *Faith of the Fatherless* (San Francisco, Ignatius Press, 2015).

96. Cf. Emily Esfahani Smith, *Daily Beast*, 12/17/2012; Camille Paglia, *Break, Blow, Burn* (Vintage: 2006); Ibid., *Glittering Images: A Journey Through Art From Egypt To Star Wars* (Vintage, 2013).

97. Cf. *The Sun Sentinel*, Fort Lauderdale Edition, 1968; cf. *Religion and Philosophy*, www.city-data.com/forum/religion-philosophy/330369-deathbed-admission-atheists.

98. Nietzsche, *The Gay Science*, trans. Kaufmann (New York: Vintage, 1974), 181.

99. Albert Camus, *The Myth of Sisyphus and Other Essays* (New York: Vintage, 1991), 3.

100. *Religious Belief Systems of Persons with High Functioning Autism*, Boston College (2015).

101. See Paul Vitz, *Faith of the Fatherless* (San Francisco, Ignatius Press, 2015).

102. Antoine Lutz, "Long-term Meditators Self-Induce High-Amplitude Gamma Sychrony During Mental Practice," *Proceedings of the National Academy of Sciences USA 101*, no. 46 (November 16, 2004): 16369–73.

103. Voltaire, "Letter to the author of the three impostors," quoted in Thomas Williams, *Greater Than You Think* (New York: Faith Words, 2008).

104. *American Journal of Psychiatry* 161, 2004: 2303–2308; *World Health Organization*, December 2005; The Mental Health of Students in Higher Education, *Royal College of Psychiatrists*, 2003; Aris Study, 2001. Much of the statistics in the following section are also found in Vox Day's *The Irrational Atheist* (Dallas: BenBella, 2008).

105. Cf. The Sun Sentinel, *Fort Lauderdale Edition*, 1968; cf. *Religion and Philosophy*, www.city-data.com/forum/religion-philosophy/330369-deathbed-admission-atheists.

106. C.S. Lewis, *Mere Christianity* (San Francisco: Harper Collins, 2015), Book 3, Chapter 10.

107. http://www.peterkreeft.com/topics/desire.htm. Also, Ronald Tacelli, *Handbook of Christian Apologetics: Hundreds of Answers to Crucial Questions* (Downers Grove, IVP Academic, 1994), 49f.

108. Cf. Rene Descartes, *Meditations and Other Metaphysical Writings* (New York: Penguin Classics, 1999), *Third Meditation*; Cf. Lawrence Nolan, *Stanford Encyclopedia of Philosophy*, April 12, 2011, plato.stanford.edu/entries/Descartes-ontological; Adam, Charles, and Paul Tannery. 1964–1976. *Oeuvres de Descartes*, vols. I-XII, revised edition. Paris: J. Vrin/C.N.R.S; Cottingham, John, Robert Stoothoff, Dugald Murdoch, and (for vol. 3) Anthony Kenny, eds. and trans. 1984. *The Philosophical Writings of Descartes*, vols. 1–3 (Cambridge: Cambridge University Press, 1984); Ibid. "Meditations on First Philosophy," in *The Philosophical Works of Descartes*, edited and trans. Elizabeth Haldane (Cambridge: Cambridge University Press, 1931).

109. Andrew Newberg, Eugene D'Aquili and Vince Rause, *Why God Won't Go Away: Brain Science and the Biology of Belief* (New York: Ballantine Books, 2001), 145–6, 113.

110. Einstein, "The World as I See It, 1931," in *Forum and Century*, vol. 84, 193.

111. Andrew Newberg, Eugene D'Aquili and Vince Rause, *Why God Won't Go Away: Brain Science and the Biology of Belief* (New York: Ballantine Books, 2001), 145–6, 113.

112. Mario Beauregard, *The Spiritual Brain* (New York: HarperOne, 2007), 99.

113. Francis Crick, *The Astonishing Hypothesis: The Scientific Search for the Soul* (New York: Touchtone, 1995), 262; Steve Pinker, *How the Mind Works* (New York: Norton, 1997), 305. Given the evolutionary process, the experience of the transcendental is beneficial for the survival of the species as a whole. If God exists or does not, those who oppose a belief in God are hurting the species.

114. Karl Marx, *On Religion*, ed. and trans. Saul K. Padover (New York: McGraw Hill, 1974), 41.

115. Cf. Beauregard, 37.

116. James W. Fowler, *Stages of Faith* (New York: HarperOne 1995), cited in Vost, 91.

117. Beauregard, 272.

118. See John Pasquini, *The Existence of God* (University Press of America, 2010); *Atheist Persona: Causes and Consequences* (New York: University Press of America, 2014).

119. Cf. John Henry Newman, *An Essay in Aid of Grammar of Assent* (Westminster Classics, 1973), 109–10.

120. See John Pasquini, *The Existence of God* (University Press of America, 2010); *Atheist Persona: Causes and Consequences* (New York: University Press of America, 2014).

121. Antoine Lutz, "Long-term Meditators Self-Induce High-Amplitude Gamma Sychrony During Mental Practice," *Proceedings of the National Academy of Sciences USA 101*, no. 46 (November 16, 2004): 16369-73.

122. Thomas Aquinas quotes come from *Summa Theologiae: A Concise Translation*, ed. And trans. Timothy McDermott (Westminster: Christian Classics, 1989); (Pt. I, Q. 2, Art. 3).

123. Peter Kreeft, *The Summa of the Summa* (San Francisco: Ignatius Press, 1990), 63; (Pt. I, Q. 2, Art. 3).

124. Augustine, *On Free Choice and the Will*. Translated by Anna S. Benjamin and L. H. Hackstaff (New York: Bobbs-Merrill).

125. Cf. Bjorn Brembs, *Royal Society Journal*. rsp.royalsocitypublishing.org/ content/ early/ 2010 /12 /14 /4spb.2010.2325. An extensive bibliography regarding the study of neuroscience and free will can be found in the full published article.

126. Cf. "That a Most Perfect Being Exists" (*Quod ens perfectissimum existit*, 1676) A VI iii 578/SR 101; Ibid., 53/SR 107) in *Stanford Encyclopedia of Philosophy*.

127. The above argument is influenced by Charles Hartshorne's interpretation of Anselm's ontological argument, *Anselm's Argument* (LaSalle: Open Court, 1965).The ontological argument for the existence of God is one that has been fervently argued over: in more recent times, Goebel and Alvin Plantinga have developed versions of Anselm's argument. I personally do not find them convincing, but I offer the names of Goebel and Plantinga up for further exploration.

128. Augustine's theory from the mind to God, which shares similarities to Anselm's Ontological Argument, has been refashioned into a new argument.

129. John Pasquini, *Atheist Persona* (Lanham: UPA, 2014), 21; *The Free Press*, 6/6/2010, www.thefreepressonline.co.uk/news/1/1830.htm, *Nairaland Forum*, www.nairaland.com/746723/famous-atheists-last-words-before; *Godtube*, Liberty University, www.godtube.com/watch/?v=wlykl7nx;; *Religion and Philosophy*, www.city-data.com/forum/religion-philosophy/330369-deathbed-admission-atheists.

130. One of the great intellectual works of all time is attributed to Blaise Pascal, *Pensees*, trans. W.F. Trotter (New York: E.P. Dutton and Company, 1958).

131. Karl Rahner, S.J., *Foundations of Christian Faith* (New York: Herder and Herder, 2012), 402.

Bibliography

Adler, Mortimer. *Philosopher at Large*. New York: Macmillan, 1977.

Archer, S.L. "Gender Differences in Identity Development." *Journal of Adolescence* 12 (1989).

Aquinas, Thomas. *Summa Theologiae: A Concise Translation*, ed. and trans. Timothy McDermott. Westminster: Christian Classics, 1989.

———. *Summa Contra Gentiles—Book One*. Translated by Anton C. Pegis. New York: Doubleday, 1955.

———. *Treatise on Happiness*. Translated by Vernon J. Bourke. Garden City, NY: Image.

———. *Aquinas on Being and Essence*. Translated and commentated by Joseph Bobik. Notre Dame: University of Notre Dame Press, 1965.

———. *On Being and Essence*. Translated by Armand Maruer. Toronto: The Pontifical Institute of Mediaeval Studies, 1968.

Aristotle. *The Basic Works of Aristotle*. Edited by Richard McKeon. New York: Random House, 1941.

Baker, Maggie. "Vestigial Organs Not So Useless After All." *National Geographic News*. October 28, 2010.

Barbour, Ian. *Religion in the Age of Science*. London: SCM Press, 1990.

———. *When Science Meets Religion*. London: SPCK, 2000.

Barr, Stephen. *Modern Physics and Ancient Faith*. Notre Dame: University of Notre Dame Press, 2003.

Barrow, J.D. *The Anthropic Cosmological Principle*. Oxford: Oxford University Press, 1986.

Beit-Hallahmi, Benjamin. "Atheist: A Psychological Profile." In *The Cambridge Companion to Atheism*.

Berman, David. *A History of Atheism in Britain*. London: Croom Helm, 1988.

Berman, Harold. *Law and Revolution*. Cambridge: Harvard University Press, 1983.

Beauregard, Mario. *The Spiritual Brain*. New York: HarperOne, 2007.

Behe, Michael. *Darwin's Black Box*. New York: Free Press, 2006.

———. William Dembski, Stephen Meyer, *Science and Evidence for Design in the Universe*. San Francisco: Ignatius, 2000.

———. *The Edge of Evolution*. New York: Free Press, 2006.

Boekraad, Adrian and Tristram, Henry. *The Argument from Conscience to the Existence of God*. London: Mill Hill, 1961.

Bojowald, Martin. "What Happened Before the Big Bang?" *Nature Physics* (July 1, 2007); 523–25.

Bowlby, John. *The Making and Breaking of Affectional Bonds*, 1979.

Bradley, Walter. "The 'Just So' Universe." In Dembski and Kushiner, *Signs of Intelligence*. Grand Rapids: Brazos Press, 2001.

Baluffi, Cajetan. *The Charity and the Church*. Trans. Denis Gargan. Dublin: Gill and Son, 1885.

Brzezinski, Zbigniew. *Out of Control*. New York: Touchstone, 1995.

Buckley, Michael. *At the Origins of Modern Atheism*. London: Yale University Press, 1987.

Bullock, Alan. *Hitler: A Story in Tyranny*. HarperPrennial Edition, 1991.

Burke, Theresa. *Forbidden Grief*. Springfield: Acorn Books, 2002.

Burkert, Walter. *Ancient Mystery Cults*. Cambridge: Harvard University Press, 1987.

Campbell, Robert. *Campbell's Psychiatric Dictionary*. Oxford: Oxford University Press, 2003.

Camus, Albert. *The Myth of Sisyphus and Other Essays*. New York: Vintage, 1991.

Caplan, A.L. Ed. *Darwin, Marx, and Freud: Their Influence on Moral Theology*. New York: UP, 1984.

Carroll-Cruz, Joan. *Mysteries Marvels and Miracles in the Lives of the Saints*. Illinois: TAN Books, 1997.

Chalmers, David. *The Conscious Mind*. Oxford University Press, 1996.

Clark, Kenneth. *Civilization: A Personal View. New York*: HarperPerennial, 1969.

Clark, M. "Nietzsche's Immoralism and the Concept of Morality." In *Nietzsche, Genealogy, Morality*. Essays on Nietzsche's 'Genealogy of Morals.' Ed. R. Schacht, 15–34.

Clowes, Brian. *The Facts of Life*. Front Royal, 2001.

Cole, Susan. *Theo Mgaloi*. Leiden: Brill, 1984.

Coleman, Andrew, Ed. *A Dictionary of Psychology*. Oxford: Oxford University Press, 2007.

Conway, David. *The Rediscovery of Wisdom*. London: Macmillan, 2000.

Comstock, G. *Television in America*. Newbury Park: Sage Publications, 1991.

Crick, Francis. *The Astonishing Hypothesis: The Scientific Search for the Soul*. New York: Touchtone, 1995.

———. *Life Itself*. New York: Simon and Schuster, 1988.

———. *What Mad Pursuit*. New York: Basic Books, 1988.

Daly, Lowrie. *The Medieval University*. New York: Sheed and Ward, 1961.

Darwin, Charles. *On the Origin of Species*. Cambridge: Harvard University Press, 1964.

Darwin, Francis, ed., *The Life and Letters of Charles Darwin*. Vol. 2. New York: Appleton, 1888.

Darrow, Clarence. *The Story of My Life*. New York: Da Capo Press, 1996.

Davey, Graham, Ed. *Encyclopedic Dictionary of Psychology*. Oxford: Oxford University Press, 2005.

Davis, Michael. *For Altar and Throne*. St. Paul: Remnant, 1997.

Dawkins, Richard. *River Out of Eden: A Darwinian View of Life*. New York: Basic, 1995.

———. *The Blind Watchmaker*. New York: Norton, 1986.

———. *The God Delusion*. Boston: Houghton Mufflin, 2006.

Day, Vox. *The Irrational Atheist*. Dallas: Benbella Books, Inc., 2008.

de Beauvoir, Simone. *Memoirs of a Dutiful Daughter*. Trans. J. Kirkup. Cleveland: World Publishing, 1959.

Deamer, David. "The First Living Systems: A Bioenergetic Perspective." *Microbiology and Molecular Biology Reviews*, 61:239 (1997).

Dembski, William. *Intelligent Design*. Dover Grove: Inter Varsity, 1999.

———. *Intelligent Design Uncensored*. Downers Grove: IVP Books, 2010.

———. *The Design Inference*. Cambridge: Cambridge University Press, 1998.

———. Jonathan Wells. *The Design of Life. Dallas: Foundations for Thought and Ethics*, 2007.

Dennett, Daniel. *Breaking the Spell*. New York: Penguin Books, 2007.

Dennis, Brandon. "Beauty, Truth and Morality." *The Daily of the University of Washington*. February 22, 2007.

Denton, Michael. *Evolution: A Theory in Crisis*. Chevy Chase: Adler and Adler, 1986.

Descartes, Rene. "Meditations on First Philosophy," in *The Philosophical Words of Descartes*. Edited and translated by Elizabeth S. Haldane and Ross. Cambridge: Cambridge University Press, 1931.

Diamant, Anita. "Media Violence." *Parents*. October 1994: 40–5.

Dose, Klaus. "The Origin of Life: More Questions and Answers." *Interdisciplinary Science Reviews* (1988): 13, 348.

Durant, Will. *The Story of Philosophy*. New York: Garden City Publishing, 1938.

Dyson, Freeman. *Disturbing the Universe*. New York: Harper and Row, 1979.

Dziwisz, Stanislaw. *A Life with Karol: My Forty-Year Friendship with the Man Who Became Pope*. New York: Doubleday, 2008.

Eagleton, Terry. "Lunging, Flailing, Mispunching: A Review of Richard Dawkins' The God Delusion," *London Review of Books*, October 19, 2006.

Eccles, John. *The Evolution of the Brain*. New York: Routledge, 1989.

Einstein, Albert. *Ideas and Opinions*. Trans. Sonja Bargmann. New York: Dell, 1973.

———. Lettres a Maurice Solovine reproduits en facsimile et traduits en francais. Paris: Gauthier-Vilars, 1956.

———. "The World as I See It," *In Forum and Century*. Vol. 84, 1931, 193.

Eldredge, Niles. *Reinventing Darwin*. New York: Wiley, 1995

Ellis, Albert. *Reason and Emotion in Psychotherapy*. New York: Birch Lane Press, 1994.

———. *Rational, Emotive Behavior Therapy: It Works for Me*. New York: Prometheus Books, 2004.

Ferguson, John. *The Religions of the Roman Empire*. Ithaca: Cornell University Press, 1970.

Flew, Antony. "My Pilgrimage from Atheism to Theism." *Philosophia Christi*. Vol. 6. No. 2. 2004, 201.

Fowler, James. *Stages of Faith*. New York: HarperOne 1995.

Frankl, Victor. *The Doctor and the Soul: From Psychotherapy to Logotherapy*. New York: Vintage, 1973.

Franklin, Howard. *The Way of the Cell*. New York: Oxford University Press, 2001.

Freud, Sigmund. *Leonardo da Vinci*. New York: Random House, 1947.

Frey-Wysslilng, A. *Comparative Organellography of the Cytoplasm*. New York: Springer-Verlang, 1973.

Feuerbach, Ludwig. *Lectures on the Essence of Religion*. Trans. Ralph Manheim, New York: Harper and Row Publishers, 1967.

Genovesi, Vincent. *In Pursuit of Love, 2nd ed*. Collegeville: The Liturgical Press, 1996.

Gerhard Ulhorn, Gerhard. *Christian Charity in the Ancient Church*. New York: Charles Scribner's Sons, 1883.

Gimpel, Jean. *The Medieval Machine: The Industrial Revolution of the Middle Ages*. New York: Holt, Rinehart, and Winston, 1976.

Godwin, Joscelyn. *Mystery Religion in the Ancient World. Ithaca*. Cornell University Press, 1971.

Goodell, Henry. "The Influence of the Monks in Agriculture." In *Goodell Papers, University of Massachusetts*.

Gould, Stephen. "Punctuated Equilibria: An Alternative to Phyletic Gradualism." In *Models of Paleobiology,* ed. T.J.M. Schopf. San Francisco: Freeman, Cooper and Co., 1972: 82–115.

Graham Ryken, Philip. *Jeremiah and Lamentations: From Sorrow to Hope*. Wheaton: Crossway, 2001.

Gray, John. Straw Dogs: *Thoughts on Humans and Other Animals*. London: Granta Books, 2002.

Gregoire, Reginald. *The Monastic Realm*. New York: Rizzoli, 1985.

Halvorson, Richard. "Questioning the Orthodoxy: Intelligent Design Theory Is Breaking the Scientific Monopoly of Darwinism." *Harvard Political Review* (May 14): 2002.

Hanke, Lewis. *All Mankind is One*. DeKalb: Northern Illinois University Press, 1974.

Harris, Sam. *Letter to a Christian Nation*. New York: Knopf, 2006.

Hayman, Ronald. *Nietzsche: A Critical Life*. New York: Oxford University Press, 1980.

Hedley Brooke, John Hedley. *Science and Religion: Some Historical Perspectives*. Cambridge: University Press, 1991.

Heilbron, J. L. *Annual Invitation Lecture to the Scientific Instrument Society*. Royal Institution, London, December 6, 1995.

Helmstader, Richard. *Freedom and Religion in the 19th Century*. Stanford University Press, 1997.

Bibliography

Herbert, Nick. *The Elemental Mind*. UK: Dutton, 1993.

Hick, John. *The New Frontier of Religion and Science: Religious Experience, Neuroscience, and the Transcendent*. Bassingstoke: Palgrave Macmillan, 2006.

Hitchens, Christopher. *god is not Great*. New York: Twelve, 2009.

Inzlicht, Michael. *Psychological Science. University of Toronto*. March 4, 2009.

Israel, Johnathan. *Enlightenment Contested...Emancipation of Man*. Oxford: Oxford University Press, 2006.

———. *Radical Enlightenment*. Oxford: Oxford University Press, 2001.

Jastrow, Robert. *God and the Astronomers*. New York: W.W. Norton, 1992. Second edition.

Jones, J.W. *Contemporary Psychoanalysis and Religion*. New Haven: Yale University Press, 1991.

Jurgens, William. *The Faith of the Early Fathers*. Vol. 1. Collegeville: The Liturgical Press, 1970.

Kant, Immanuel. *Critique of Pure Reason*. Translated by Norman Smith. New York: St. Martin's Press, 1965.

Kasper, Walter. *The God of Jesus Christ*. Trans. Matthew J. O'Connell. New York: Crossroad Publishing, 1992.

Kasun, Jacqueline. *War Against Population*. San Francisco: Ignatius Press, 1999.

Kaufman, Walter. *Basic Writings of Nietzsche*. New York: The Modern Library, 1992.

———. *The Portable Nietzsche*. New York: Penguin Books, 1968.

Kalvelage, Francis Mary. *Padre Pio: The Wonder Worker*. San Francisco: Ignatius Press, 2005.

Kirsch, Adam. "If men are from Mars, What's God?" *New York Sun*. February 8, 2006.

Kluger, Jeffrey. "Is God in Our Genes?" *Time*. October 25, 2004.

Knowles, David. *The Evolution of Medieval Thought. 2nd ed*. London: Longman, 1988.

Koerbel, Pam. *Abortions' Second Victim*. Wheaton: Victor Books, 1986.

Kors, A.C. *D'Holbach's Coterie*. Princeton: Princeton University Press.

Kubler-Ross, Elisabeth. *Death and Dying*. New York: Macmillan, 1993.

Kung, Hans. *Freud and the Problem of God*. New Haven: Yale University Press, 1990.

Kwitny, Jonathan. *Man of the Century: The Life and Times of Pope John Paul II*. New York: Henry Holt and Company, 1997.

Langford, Jerome. *Galileo, Science and the Church*. New York: Desclee, 1966.

Lecky, William. *History of European Morals*. Vol. 1. New York: Appleton and Co., 1870.

Leiter, B. *Nietzsche on Morality*. London, 2002.

Lewontin, Richard. "Billions of Billions of Demons." Review of Carl Sagan: *The Haunted World—New York Review of Books*. January, 9, 1997, 37.

Lockwood, Michael. *Mind, Brain and the Quantum*. Basil Blackwell, 1989.

Lynch, Joseph. *The Medieval Church*. London: Longman, 1992.

MacDonnell, Joseph. *Jesuit Geometers*. St. Louis: Institute of Jesuit Sources, 1989. Appendix 1, 6-7.

Mackay, Donald. *Brains, Machines and Persons*. Grand Rapids: Eerdmans, 1980.

Macintyre, Ben. *Forgotten Fatherland*. Uk: Pan Books, 1993.

Marx, Karl. "Contribution to the Critique of Hegel's Philosophy of Right." Quoted in Walter Kasper, *The God of Jesus Christ*. New York: Crossroad Publishing, 1992.

———. *On Religion*, Ed. and Trans. Saul K. Padover. New York: McGraw Hill, 1974.

McCullogh, Larson. "Religious Involvement and Mortality." *Health Psychology* 19, 3, 211–222.

McGrath, Alister. *The Dawkins Delusion*. Downers Grove: IVP, 2007.

———. *Why God Won't Go Away*. Nashville: Thomas Nelson, 2010.

———. *Science and Religion: An Introduction*. Oxford: Blackwell Publishers, 1999.

———. *The Twilight of Atheism: The Rise and Fall of Disbelief in the Modern World*. London: Rider, 2005.

McKown, Delos. *The Classical Marxist Critiques of Religion: Marx, Engels, Lenin, Kautsky*. The Hague: Martinus Nijhoff, 1975.

Medawar, Peter B. *The Limits of Science*. Oxford: Oxford University Press, 1985.

Meissner, W.W. *Psychoanalysis and Religious Experience*. New Haven: Yale University Press, 1984.

Meyer, Marvin. Ed. *Sacred Texts of the Mystery Religions: A Sourcebook*. Philadelphia: University of Pennsylvania Press, 1999.

Milton, Richard. *Shattering the Myths of Darwinism*. Rochester: Park Street Press, 1997.

Minois, Georges. *Histoire de L'atheisme*. La Fleche: Fayard, 1993.

Moeller, Charles. "The Theology of Unbelief." *Concilium: Theology in the Age of Renewal*. 23. February 1967: 35.

Molnar, Thomas. "Jean-Paul Sartre: A Late Return." *National Review* 34. June 11, 1982: 677.

Monod, Jacques. *Chance and Necessity: An Essay on the Natural Philosophy of Modern Biology*. London: Collins, 1972.

Mortimer, Jeffrey. "How TV Violence Hits Kids." *The Education Digest*. October 1994: 16-19.

Murray, W.J. *My Life Without God*. Nashville: Thomas Nelson, 1982.

Nelso, Marcia. "Bestsellers from the Academy." *Publisher's Weekly* 253. No. 46 (November 2006): 20.

Newberg, Andrew. *Scientific American*. January 16, 2012.

———. *Why God Won't Go Away: Brain Science and the Biology of Belief*. New York: Ballantine Books, 2001.

Newman, John Henry Cardinal. *Essays and Sketches*. Vol. 3. Ed. Charles Harrold. New York: Longmans, Green and Co., 1948.

Nielsen, Kal. *Ethics without God*. Buffalo: Prometheus Books, 1990.

Nietzsche, Frederick. *The Gay Science*. Trans. Kaufmann. New York: Vintage, 1974.

O'Leary, Denyse. *By Design or by Chance*. Minneapolis: Augsburg, 2004.

Paglia, Camille. *Break, Blow, Burn*. Vintage: 2006.

———. *Glittering Images: A Journey Through Art From Egypt To Star Wars*. Vintage, 2013.

Paloutzian, Raymond. "Psychology, the Human Science, and Religion." In *The Oxford Handbook of Religion and Science*, Ed. Philip Clayton. Oxford: Oxford University Press, 2006.

Peacocke, A.R. *Theology for a Scientific Age—Being and Becoming*. Minneapolis: Fortress Press, 1993.

Pennington, Kenneth. "The History of Rights in Western Thought." *Emory Law Journal* 47 (1998): 327-52.

Pinker, Steve. *How the Mind Works*. New York: Norton, 1997.

Polkinghome, John. *Belief in God in an Age of Science*. London: Yale University Press, 2003.

Pantinga, Alvin. *Faith and Philosophy*. Grand Rapids: Eerdmans, 1964.

Popper, Karl and John Eccles, *The Self and Its Brain*. London: Routledge, 1990.

———. "Christianity and Science." In *Oxford Handbook of Religion and Science*. Ed. Philip Clayton. Oxford University Press, 2006.

———. *Faith, Science and Understanding*. New Haven: Yale University Press, 2000.

Pospielovsky, Dimitry. *A History of Marxist-Leninist Atheism*. London: Macmillan, 1987.

Radin, Dean. *The Conscious Universe*. San Francisco: HarperSanFrancisco, 1997.

Raines, John. *Marx on Religion*. Philadelphia: Temple University Press, 2002.

Rana, Fazale. *The Cell's Design*. Grand Rapids: Baker Books, 2008.

Rand, Ayn. *The Fountainhead*. New York: Signet, 1971.

Reardon, David. *Aborted Women—Silent No More*. Westchester: Crossway Books, 1987.

Rega, Frank. *Padre Pio and America*. TAN Books, 2005.

Reiser, Paul and Teri. *Help for Post-Abortion Women*. Grand Rapids: Zondervan, 1989.

Rizzuto, A.M. *The Birth of the Living God*. Chicago: University of Chicago Press, 1979.

Robinson, Richard. *An Atheist's Values*. Oxford: Blackwell, 1975.

Ross, Alexander. "Spiritual Suicide." *The Catholic Social Science Review VIII*. (2003): 2007–222.

Ross, Hugh. *The Creator and the Cosmos*. Colorado Springs: NavPress, 2001.

Rothland, Murray. *An Austrian Perspective on the History of Economic Thought*. Hants: Edward Elgar, 1995.

Ruffin, Bernard. *Padre Pio: The True Story*. Our Sunday Visitor, 1991.

Runes, Dagobert, Ed. *Dictionary of Philosophy*. Savage: Littlefield, Inc., 1983.

Russell, Bertrand. *Why I am Not a Christian*. New York: Simon and Schuster, 1957.

Sanchez-Sorondo, Marcelo. *Vitoria, The Original Philosopher of Rights in Hispanic Philosophy in the Age of Discovery*. Kevin White. Ed. Washington: Catholic University of America Press, 1997.

Sanger, Margaret. *The Cruelty of Charity*. Swarthmore College Library Edition.

———. *The Pivot of Civilization*. Michael Perry. Ed. Seattle: Inkling Books, 2001.

———. *Women, Morality, and Birth Control*. New York: New York Publishing, 1922.

———, *The Woman Rebel*. Vol. 1. No. 1. Reprinted in *Woman in the New Race*. New York: Brentanos Publishers, 1922.

Satir. P. "How Cilia Move." *Scientific American* (1974): 231 (4), 44–52.

Scharfenberg, Joachim. *Sigmund Freud and His Critique of Religion*. Philadelphia: Fortress Press, 1988.

Schmidt, Alvin. *Under the Influence: How Christianity Transformed Civilization*. Grand Rapids: Zondervan, 2001.

Schumpeter, Joseph. *History of Economic Analysis*. New York: Oxford University Press, 1954.

Schroeder, Windred. *Moralischer Nihilismus*. Stuttgart: Reclam, 2005.

Scott, James. *The Spanish Origin of International Law*. Washington: Georgetown University Press, 1928.

Shermer, Michael. *How We Believe*. New York: Freeman, 2000.

Spero, M.H. *Religious Objects as Psychological Structures*. Chicago: University of Chicago Press, 1992.

Sperry, Roger. *Science and Moral Priority*. Oxford: Basil Blackwell, 1983.

Spilka, B. *The Psychology of Religion: An Empirical Approach*. New York: Guilford, 2003.

Spitzer, Robert. *New Proofs for the Existence of God: Contributions of Contemporary Physics and Philosophy*. Cambridge: William B. Eerdmans, 2010.

Stannard, Russell. *The God Experiment*. London: Faber and Faber, 1999.

Steven, Rose. *Against Biological Determinism*. London: Alison and Busby, 1982.

Stone, Irving. *Clarence Darrow for the Defense*. New York: Doubleday, 1941.

Strobel, Lee. *The Case for a Creator*. Grand Rapids: Zondervan, 2004.

Sullivan, R.E. *John Toland and the Deist Controversy*. Cambridge: Harvard University Press, 1982.

Tierney, Brian. *The Idea of Natural Rights*. Grand Rapids: William Eerdmans, 2001.

Thrower, James. *A Short History of Western Atheism*. London: Pemberton Books, 1971.

Turcan, Robert. *The Cults of the Roman Empire*. Oxford: Blackwell, 1996.

Udias, Agustin. *Searching the Heavens and the Earth: The History of Jesuit Observatories*. Dordrecht: Kluwer Academic Publishers, 2003.

Ulansey, David. *The Origins of the Mithraic Mysteries*. New York: Oxford University Press, 1989.

Varghese, Roy Abraham. "The Supreme Science." *Viewpoints*. December 16. 2004: 35A.

Vergote, Antoine. "What the Psychology of Religion Is and What It Is Not." *International Journal for the Psychology of Religion 3* (1993): 73.

Vermaseren, Maarten. *Cybele and Attis: The Myth and the Cult*. London: Thames and Hudson, 1977.

Vitz, Paul C. *The Faith of the Fatherless*. San Francisco: Ignatius Press, 2013.

Vost, Kevin. *From Atheism to Catholicism*. Huntington: Our Sunday Visitor, 210.

Vought, Jeanette. *Post Abortion Trauma*. Grand Rapids: Zondervan, 1991.

Wells, Jonathan. *Icons of Evolution*. Washington: Regnery, 2000.

———. *The Politically Incorrect Guide to Darwinism and Intelligent Design*. Washington: Regnery, 2006.

Whitehead, K.D. "Sex Education: Vatican Guidelines." *Crisis*. Vol. 13. No. 5. May, 1996.

Whitesides, George. "Revolutions in Chemistry: Priestley Medalist Address." *Chemical and Engineering News*, 85: 12-17 (March 26, 2007).

Wicks, Robert, "Arthur Schopenhauer." In *The Stanford Encyclopedia in Philosophy*. Ed. Edward Zalta, 2007.

Wiener, D. *Albert Ellis: Passionate Skeptic*. New York: Praeger, 1998.

Wilson, Edward. *On Human Nature*. Cambridge: Harvard University Press, 1978.

Woods, Thomas E. *How the Catholic Church Build Western Civilization*. Lanham: Regnery Publishing, 2005.

Woodard, Thomas. *Darwin Strikes Back*. Grand Rapids: Baker Books, 2006.

Wootton, David. "New Histories of Atheism," in *Atheism from the Reformation to the Enlightenment*. Ed. Michael Hunter. Oxford: Clarendon Press, 1992.

Word, Keith. *Pascal's Fire: Scientific Faith and Religious Understanding*. Oxford: One World, 2006.

Zacharias, Ravi. *The End of Reason*. Grand Rapids: Zondervan, 2008.